D0508419

THE HEADACHE CURE

HOW TO UNCOVER WHAT'S REALLY CAUSING YOUR PAIN AND FIND LASTING RELIEF

Joseph Kandel, M.D. & David Sudderth, M.D.

McGraw-Hill

New York   Chicago   San Francisco   Lisbon   London   Madrid   Mexico City
Milan   New Delhi   San Juan   Seoul   Singapore   Sydney   Toronto

Library of Congress Cataloging-in-Publication Data

Kandel, Joseph.
    The headache cure : how to uncover what's really causing your pain and find lasting
relief / by Joseph Kandel and David Sudderth.
        p.   cm.
    Includes bibliographical references.
    ISBN 0-07-145736-4
    1. Headache—Popular works.   I. Sudderth, David B.   II. Title.

RC392.K359   2005
616.8'491—dc22   2005007305

3 4 5 6 7 8 9 0   DOC/DOC   0 9 8 7 6

ISBN 0-07-145736-4

Interior design by Think Design Group, LLC

McGraw-Hill books are available at special quantity discounts to use as premiums and sales
promotions, or for use in corporate training programs. For more information, please write to
the Director of Special Sales, Professional Publishing, McGraw-Hill, Two Penn Plaza, New York,
NY 10121-2298. Or contact your local bookstore.

This book is printed on acid-free paper.

To my wonderful wife, who encourages,

supports, inspires, and loves me.

—Joseph Kandel

For Lucia, with love and admiration.

—David Sudderth

Contents

PART III

Migraines and Other Chronic Severe Headaches

PART IV

Getting to Wellness: Working with Your Doctor to Treat Your Headaches

Prescribing Relief: Medications That Combat and Prevent Recurring Headaches

Over-the-Counter Drugs, Vitamins, and Supplements

Acknowledgments

Dr. Kandel wishes to thank Debbie Larson, RN. She is my right hand and she works tirelessly to make sure that my patients receive the absolute best care that I can provide. And I would like to thank Angel Hjelle, who always brings a smile to the office and makes all of my patients comfortable, each and every day.

Both authors would like to thank our excellent editor, Natasha Graf, for her many very helpful suggestions and the positive feedback she has given us. We would also like to thank health writer Christine Adamec for her assistance with research and writing.

Introduction

Denise, 35, says that about half the time she feels fine. Sometimes, she even finds herself wondering if she is exaggerating how bad her headache problem really is. However, then she gets slammed with what she calls a category 5 headache, and she knows her problem is all too real—and it's all bad.

Carly, 27, suffers from severe painful headaches nearly every day. She has been to numerous doctors and tried many medications, but so far, nothing has worked. Carly was in a car accident several months ago; and it was a few days after the crash that her daily headaches started.

Tim, 43, suffers from severe headaches that occur several times a month. When they hit, he can't think clearly and has to call in sick to work. Or, if he's already at work when the headache takes over, he has to lie down until he's well enough to drive home. His headaches usually last a few hours. While this may not sound that bad, Tim says that even a few hours of torture is tough to take. His headaches are getting him into trouble at work and at home.

For these three people—and millions more across the United States—headache pain places a major strain on their lives. They need a better handle on their severe chronic headaches, and they need to make some changes in their lives in order to gain some real relief—whether these changes come through medication, physical therapy, massage therapy, and/or other treatments. All they know is that for now, headaches are running their lives. But we're here to say that it doesn't have to be that way.

Are Severe Headaches Running Your Life?

Constant severe headaches can derail your life, and the lives of the people you care about. They're a pain in the neck and sometimes, they literally *are* a pain in your neck—such as when you have a cervicogenic headache. (These are headaches that stem from neck or shoulder pain, which we describe in greater detail in Part II, Chapters 4 through 6.)

For example, you can't go out to dinner with your spouse—even though it's his birthday—because your head feels like a volcano ready to erupt. All you want to do is lie down in a dark room, pull the covers over your head, and lie very still until the worst pain has passed you by.

Or maybe it's not your husband's birthday. It's just a regular day, and you can't focus enough to read a story to your child—something that's important to both of you. Or maybe you can't take your dog for a walk in the sunshine because you feel the onset of a headache and *know* the sunlight would hurt your head far too much. Constant painful headaches can sideline a lot of your life if you let them. (You're reading this book, so that's a good first step to taking action!)

When it comes to work, you may be unable to finish an important report that the boss is counting on you to finalize. Why not? Because all you can concentrate on right now is the severe and overwhelming pain from your headache. In fact, you probably think that you have a migraine, and maybe you're right. However, even if you're wrong, the fact is that you have a severe headache—and if it's happening frequently, you need help.

We're two neurologists who have treated thousands of patients with chronic severe headaches. Some of our new patients have been in such despair over their chronic severe headaches that we found them plunged into a severe depression. They felt like their lives were governed by a sort of malevolent headache god, and they had no way of knowing how to fend off this evil demon who ruled their lives. They felt out of control, never knowing when a headache would strike. The good news is that there are plenty of things that you *can* do. So keep on reading!

Getting to the Source of Your Pain

In this first section, we help you understand headaches in general, and your own headache type in particular. We provide an overview of key information on chronic headaches and offer a self-test to help you determine the severity of your headaches. We include a self-evaluation to help you discover the type of headaches you may have (migraines, cervicogenic, tension-type, or other type). Your current diagnosis may be wrong, which is why your headache treatments aren't working or aren't working as well as you would like. Based on your responses, we recommend must-read chapters for you and offer guidelines on finding a new physician, if needed. Finally, you'll find out about the major headache triggers (such as weather and foods) and you'll do a self-evaluation to help you zero in on triggers you may not even know you have.

CHAPTER 1

What You Need to Know About Severe Chronic Headaches

Remember these three key points as you read this book: chronic severe headaches are real, they're not your fault, and your headache pain problem can nearly always be improved. When you suffer with chronic severe headaches and you can't find any relief, it's common to start believing the problem might be "all in your head." You know that it really hurts when the pain is actively present, but when the headache's gone, you worry that maybe you've exaggerated the pain. Unfortunately, many sufferers believe that chronic headaches are their own fault—whether they think they know *how* they caused them or not. Other patients have suffered so long with headaches that they've nearly given up hope of full recovery. They don't even know what it is like *not* to have headache pain. If this sounds like you, do not despair—keep reading!

Chronic Headaches Are Real

Headaches may not show up as an interesting finding to neurologists like us on a *computerized tomography (CT)* scan or a *magnetic resonance imaging (MRI)* scan, and all your laboratory tests may come back saying that you're "in the normal range" of whatever was tested. However, if you are part of the population with chronic severe headaches, it doesn't matter: your pain is real.

One strange thing about pain is that, once it's gone, you rarely remember exactly what it felt like. You remember you *had* pain and what it caused you to do (lie down) or *not* do (finish an important report). However, you can't actually reexperience pain, and this pain amnesia is largely a good thing. On the other hand, sometimes it causes people to doubt themselves later, when the pain has subsided. You wonder, was it really that bad? Did I overreact? If you're like most people, the answer is no, you didn't.

But maybe you're not the one who's the doubting Thomas. Maybe you know your headaches are real, and it's others who are dubious. They may be skeptical, thinking, Nobody could have this many headaches! They don't have the problem themselves, and they may think you're exaggerating or even faking it altogether.

Unfortunately, sometimes even doctors are doubtful about chronic headaches and think that most people with this problem are neurotic. If you are having this issue with your doctor, you need to find another physician. Most doctors know that headache pain is real, and you deserve one of the good guys.

We recommend neurologists for headache problems because we *are* neurologists. But we don't recommend you see just any neurologist; you want to make sure that your neurologist has an interest in headaches and headache management. Neurologists specialize in illnesses of the brain and spinal cord and treat numerous patients with headaches. But many types of doctors treat chronic headaches. (Read Chapter 2 for more information on the difference between primary care doctors and headache specialists.)

Chronic Headaches Are Not Your Fault

Nobody wants chronic severe headaches, and if you or someone you know suffers from this aggravating problem, there are practical steps you can take to feel better. For example, you can take our self-evaluation test in Chapter 2 to help you determine what type of headaches you may have, and then read Chapter 3 on headache triggers. Once you know what causes or contributes to your headaches (such as consuming eight cans of caffeinated soda a day), we provide you with suggestions for changing your behavioral patterns. For example, you should cut back on caffeinated soda—but you need to do it slowly, because going from eight to zero cans in one day is a sure way to induce a headache, and consequently, increase their frequency and severity.

We're stressing the idea of headaches *not* being your fault because so many of our patients have come in to see us blaming themselves for their pain. They tell themselves that they have a migraine because they *should have known* not to stay up so late last night, that they should have taken more breaks at work, or some other "should have known" actions that they beat themselves up over.

Ironically, this self-blame often tends to make the headache worse. It leads to stress, and guess what? Stress is a headache trigger. So don't do it. Sure, think about any possible errors, but learn from your mistakes, rather than regarding yourself as a bad person who deserves headaches because you did (or didn't) ———————————————— (fill in the blank). That attitude is self-defeating, and we want you to get rid of it.

Your Headache Pain Can Be Improved, and You *Can* Feel Better

If you've been suffering from chronic headaches for months or years, and tried many different medications and treatments, you may be skeptical about whether you can improve the situation. We understand your skepticism. But there are treatments and medications that are effective for many people and it's important to *not* give up!

For example, botulinum toxin type A, otherwise known as "Botox," wasn't used to treat headaches a few years ago. And yes, we are talking about the same Botox that when injected cosmetically can temporarily iron out facial wrinkles. Botox is also used effectively for chronic pain problems like headaches or back pain. (We discuss more about Botox used for headaches in Chapter 12.) In addition, there are other effective new treatment choices as well as older, tried-and-true methods that can help you feel significantly better. In this book, we cover every treatment that we know of that may help you with your chronic severe headache problem.

In addition, there are plenty of preventive actions you can take to keep migraines from occurring, whether taking prescribed medications or magnesium supplements (if you are slightly deficient in magnesium), cutting back on caffeine, or not eating trigger foods. Read about prescribed migraine medications in Chapter 10 and supplements in Chapter 11.

Another issue is that the source of your headaches may not have been correctly diagnosed. Perhaps you have a *cervicogenic* headache, a headache that stems from a problem in your neck, upper back, or shoulders. Cervicogenic headaches are such a major and often unrecognized problem that we've devoted all of Part II to this topic, and we strongly recommend you read these chapters. So many of our patients have been misdiagnosed with migraines, when their true underlying problem was something wrong with the neck or shoulder area, whether it was contracted muscles, a bulging disk, or an arthritic condition. And yet their excruciating pain was primarily felt in the head. When we resolved the cervicogenic problem, their headaches diminished significantly. Bottom line, in order for a treatment to work, you need a good diagnosis. Be sure to read Chapter 2, where we discuss how to find a good doctor and how doctors diagnose chronic severe headaches, so you'll know what to ask and what your physician should ask you.

Common Myths and Realities About Chronic Severe Headaches

We've said that your chronic severe headaches are real, not your fault, and can be improved. However, there are many myths about chronic headaches that we've heard over the years—some that are true, some that are partially true, and some that are completely untrue. We list a few here to help you separate the myths from reality.

Myth: Frequent Headaches Are Caused by Brain Tumors

Although a brain tumor *can* sometimes cause people to have a severe headache, the reverse isn't true. Most people with chronic severe headaches don't have a brain tumor. If your doctor suspects that you *might* have a brain tumor, she'll order an imaging test, such as an MRI or CT scan. Of course, just because you don't have a brain tumor doesn't mean you don't have a problem. We also don't want you to panic if your doctor does order an imaging test because it doesn't automatically mean you have a serious problem. These tests are used to rule out severe problems, and many doctors order them to be on the safe side.

Chronic severe headaches need to be resolved even when they aren't caused by brain tumors. Sometimes the most benign problems, from the doctor's perspective, can cause extremely severe pain.

Myth: Headaches Are Never Serious

As mentioned earlier, chronic headaches aren't always a sign of a brain tumor or a serious problem. However, sometimes severe chronic headaches *are* a sign of a major medical problem, such as a stroke, an aneurysm, or one of many other medical problems. We want to strongly emphasize that you should not agonize over what it might be, or worse, go to the Internet to try to diagnose yourself or a loved one. When you have constant severe headaches, see your doctor. Also, if you develop a severe headache unlike one you've ever had before, you need emergency treatment. We talk more about emergency headaches in Chapter 8.

Myth: All Severe Headaches Stem from Brain Pain

Many severe chronic headaches result from something going on in the brain. However, as we mentioned in the Introduction, cervicogenic headaches are caused by contracted muscles in the neck, shoulders, or upper spine; or by other problems that are generated in the neck, upper back, and shoulder area, such as arthritis or a back disk problem.

Some headaches are caused by a metabolic disorder, like diabetes or thyroid disease. In addition, medications can cause some chronic headaches. (We know, we know. You take medicine to get better and it gives you another problem. It doesn't seem fair.) Still other headaches are caused by infections or other illnesses. We talk more about headaches stemming from illnesses, such as hypertension, thyroid disease, diabetes, infections, and other causes, in Chapter 9.

Myth: Relax and Your Headaches Will Subside

There's *some* truth to the myth that relaxing helps headaches, in that relaxation therapy may be effective at *preventing* headaches. However, a lack of relaxation doesn't cause most chronic severe headaches. In addition, once a headache has started, you could do biofeedback or breathing exercises expertly and, in many cases, your headache still wouldn't go away. It's sort of like a toddler in the middle of having a major temper tantrum. Maybe you could have taken action earlier to stop your baby from being overtired, but it's too late and she's having a five-alarm tantrum. Similarly, you must deal with the here and now of your severe headache. Often you need medications or other therapies to bring your head pain down to a tolerable level, where relaxation might give you further relief. You will find more detailed information about relaxation therapy, acupuncture, physical therapy, massage therapy, and other non-medication therapies in Chapter 13.

Myth: Our Culture Causes Headaches

There may be a little truth to this myth, which is why it's so easy to believe. With today's busy culture of cell phones, pagers, faxes, and e-mails, life is a constant series of hurry-up events. Some people are prone to headaches and others aren't, despite our culture and how it works. This means that when stressed, you may get a headache (or a worse headache) if you're prone to them, while your spouse may get a stomachache, if that's his weak spot. Everyone is different.

Many people think that tension headaches are solely caused by excess stress, but they are actually caused by tensed-up muscles in the head and neck and have a variety of causes. Read Chapter 8 for more information on tension headaches.

Myth: Headaches Are Caused by Excessive Carbohydrates

The late Dr. Atkins may have been right that a diet high in carbohydrates (carbs) isn't healthy. However, some people have demonized carbohydrates to the extent that they are condemned as guilty for causing not only obesity but also headaches, stomachaches, and other ailments. Here's the reality. If you have a food sensitivity, such as lactose intolerance, you may get a headache from drinking milk. Or, if you're sensitive to caffeine, too much cola and/or chocolate may send you into Headache Land. But eating food with a few grams of carbohydrates usually won't trigger a severe headache in most people.

That said, it's important to realize that for many people, eating anything with chocolate or drinking red wine (or drinking hot chocolate and eating food containing red wine) may trigger a painful headache. Some people can develop a headache—fast—when they consume food prepared with food additives, such as monosodium glutamate (MSG). Some people find that a low-carb diet decreases the number of their headaches. Read more about food triggers in Chapter 3.

Myth: Women Get More Headaches Than Men

In this case, the myth is a reality—women *do* get more headaches than men. About two-thirds of our headache patients are female, and this is typical for physicians nationwide. According to the Centers for Disease Control and Prevention (CDC), about 31 million adults age 18 and older in the United States suffer from severe headaches or migraines. Of these patients, 21 million are female.

Women are more prone to suffering from nearly every headache type there is, with the exception of cluster headaches, a severe form of headache that men are more likely to experience. It's unclear why men get most cluster headaches; it could be a testosterone-related issue or something else altogether that is yet to be discovered. (Of course, women can get cluster headaches, too.) No one knows why women get more headaches, although theories abound. It could be hormonal levels or neurochemical levels. Some women get migraines around their menstrual cycle and other women get them when they're pregnant or they stop getting them when they're pregnant or after menopause. These headaches may be caused by excessive or fluctuating hormones, which throw the system off. Some researchers believe it is not just the amount of hormone but also the rapid rate of the hormone change that is the major culprit. Read more about hormonal headaches in Chapter 7 on migraines.

Myth: Severe Headaches Are Always Hereditary

Chronic severe headaches "run in" families; however, some people develop severe headaches or migraines even though their parents never had them. If you suffer from chronic severe headaches that fit the profile for migraines, even if your parents are usually headache-free, you probably are a *migraineur* (a fancy word for someone with migraine headaches), although it's always possible you've been misdiagnosed.

A Self-Evaluation: How Bad *Are* Your Headaches?

Is it fair to say that your headaches are both chronic and severe? You probably think so, since you're reading this book, but take our brief self-evaluation in this section. Of course, you'll need to see a physician in order to obtain a professional medical evaluation.

Answer "yes" or "no" to each question and read our analysis of your responses.

1. On average, I have about three or more headaches per week.
2. On a scale of 1 to 10, about half or more of my headaches are a 6 or worse.
3. I'm getting more headaches now than a year or two ago.
4. My headaches are affecting me at work.
5. My headaches are affecting me at home.
6. I'm having less sex now than a year ago, because of my headaches.
7. I regularly carry a purse, briefcase, backpack, or other object that weighs more than 15 or 20 pounds.
8. I plan my daily activities around my headaches.
9. I think of my headache pain more than 50 percent of the time.
10. My friends are tired of asking about or hearing about my headaches.

Questions 1–3: Frequency and Severity

Now, what do your answers mean? Let's take a look at the first question. If you're having three or more headaches a week, you definitely need to take action. Most people have a few headaches a year or a few headaches a month at most. Even when these headaches are severe, they can be tolerated. However, three or more headaches a week are beyond the normal level of toleration. In fact, even one severe headache per week ("only" totaling about 52 per year) is well beyond normal.

What about the level of pain that your headaches cause you, as asked in the second question? If most of your headaches are very severe (if you've rated them at a "6" and above) then that is cause for concern. We cannot emphasize enough that if you haven't seen a physician about your severe headaches, you need to see one as soon as possible. So make an appointment!

Many people find themselves trapped in a sort of headache quagmire, where they're getting more severe headaches than in the past and they can't seem to get out of this sinking quicksand of pain. If you've answered "yes" to question 3, then obviously, something is wrong. Again, you need to work with your doctor to root out the possible cause of your headaches and identify some good solutions. Maybe you're reading this book because you're concerned that the frequency of your headaches is escalating, as asked in the third question. Lorna came to see us because she was getting headaches four or five times a week, compared to two or three times a month a year ago. This is abnormal, and it's a situation requiring a medical evaluation. It doesn't necessarily mean that there's a serious problem. On the other hand, a potential serious medical problem should also be ruled out, to be on the safe side.

Questions 4–6: Affecting Work and Home Life

Did you answer "yes" to whether your headaches are affecting you at work, as asked in the fourth question? If you did, you are certainly not alone! In a study reported in 2003 in the *Journal of the American Medical Association*, researchers ponderously analyzed the loss of productive time at work in nearly 29,000 adults. They found that over the course of just two weeks, the most common pain problem reported by workers taking time off from work was headache (5.4 percent), followed by back pain (3.2 percent), and then arthritis (2 percent). Of course not everyone with a headache has a chronic problem. But if you are one of the many people who suffer from chronic headaches, it's time to act.

Many people report that their headaches are hurting them on the home front, whether it's with their partners, their children, other family members, or their friends. (And sometimes it's "all of the above.") If you responded "yes" to the fifth question, you are definitely not alone. Friends and family who don't suffer from chronic severe headaches may sometimes think that "I have a bad headache" is really code for "I don't want to be with you," or worse, "I don't like you/love you anymore." As a result, it's important for you to make sure that other people that you care about (family members, friends, coworkers, and whoever else matters to you) are all clear that you really do suffer from chronic severe headaches. Open communication can help you avoid compounding your headache problem with a relationship problem. For those people in your life who have only had a few or no severe headaches (as hard as that is to believe) it's important to understand that while you can't make them "feel your pain," you can help them to understand. One way is to compare your chronic severe headache problem with other common severe problems that many people have, such as severe back pain or chronic stomach pain. If the person you're explaining to doesn't have any chronic health problems, she probably knows someone who does, and explaining it this way may turn the lightbulb on. But for your own health, it's still important to work on resolving your chronic headaches, so tell your relative or friend you are doing so!

With regard to headaches and intimacy, as asked in question 6, we've all heard the old "Not tonight, honey, I have a headache" excuse. This is usually attributed to a wife who doesn't feel like having sex because she's tired, angry, or something else is going on. But what if a severe headache *does* prevent you from wanting to have sex, and this is becoming a problem in your relationship with your partner? Consider how many times you've had sex in the past month, and then think back to about how many times you had sex in a month a year ago. Is there a big difference now? If so, you're not alone, because many other people with chronic severe headaches share this problem with you. But it's also a problem that you (and they) need to work on. It's a shame when chronic headaches deprive people of a satisfying sexual relationship. Again, communication is the key. Follow our advice throughout this book to help you regain what was lost.

Question 7: Could Your Headache Be Another Problem?

If you're carrying a purse, backpack, or briefcase that weighs more than 15 or 20 pounds, this item could be the source of your problems. In fact, many women lug around heavy purses all day long, full of quarters, makeup, a cell phone, and so on—straining their necks and heads. Many men and women cart around heavy brief-cases full of papers, computers, and other items; and students are often loaded down with heavy backpacks. All of these things can lead to neck pain and could be the root cause of cervicogenic (neck) headaches. Eliminating many of these items could mean a major difference in the frequency and severity of your headaches.

Questions 8–10: When Headaches Interrupt Your Life

If you find that you are actually planning your daily activities around your headaches, this is a major problem. Sue, a 42-year-old stay-at-home mom, found herself in this situation. She took her two children to school each morning, but then would be limited the rest of the day by her anxiety over whether she would have a headache. If she was feeling okay, Sue would rush around to get her shopping and errands done, and then come home and collapse. Often this frantic pace would bring on a headache. If you are like Sue, read on to find out how you can take back control.

How often do you think about your headaches during the day? If you are like many of our new patients, when the pain is out of control, the answer is morning, noon, and night. But there is hope, and by learning some of the coping strategies and exercises in this book, you, too, can start thinking about more pleasant things.

Do your friends limit their conversations with you, as asked in the last question? Do they steer it away from health issues, knowing that you will bring up your headaches? Or worse, do they feel compelled to discuss your headaches with you? If you find that the answer to this question is "yes," or even "maybe," this is a major problem. To illustrate further, change the subject from headaches to something else—say, golf—and consider this example. While you might enjoy hearing about a friend's golf clubs, swing, or game occasionally, having golf as the dominant topic of conversation a majority of the time would certainly limit the friendship. Now, if that happens with "headaches," you can understand how your friends may want some space, and you can also make some changes.

The Big Picture

If you answered "yes" to at least three of the self-evaluation questions, then chronic headaches are a major factor in your life. If you answered "yes" to four or five questions, you need to realize that some changes are in order to resolve your headache problem.

What if you answered "yes" to six or more questions? Read this book and promise yourself that you're going to work with your doctor to make a plan to identify your headaches and beat them into submission. There are many medications and therapies available today, whether your problem is migraine, tension-type headache, cervicogenic headache, cluster headache, or another form. Don't accept the current situation. You can do better.

Some Basics About Headache Pain

When you suffer from severe chronic headaches, it's a good idea to have a basic understanding of what may be going on in your body, pain-wise. Some headaches are caused by pain that is from a part of the brain, while others stem from a problem that lies elsewhere in the body. There are actually a myriad of possibilities for what's causing your pain, so we'll only touch on the most prominent types of headache pain—brain pain and referred pain.

Basics About Brain Pain (Headaches Stemming from the Brain)

Sometimes headaches are caused by constricted blood vessels in the brain. Try this simple experiment. Make your hand into a very tight fist, as tight as you can manage. Feel the tenseness of the nerves and muscles and hold that position for ten seconds or so before relaxing it.

Now imagine one or more of the blood vessels in your brain as tightening up in a similar way and staying tight for hours until eventually something causes it to relax, whether it's through medication, sleep, or something else acting on your body. If you take no action, eventually a headache will usually pass, although you'll be miserable for hours or even days. We recommend treatment rather than waiting for it to pass.

You also have muscle tissue and nerves around your brain, and they may be overly tight as well—as tight as the muscles in your hand were when you made the fist. Brain pain can also be multifaceted, caused by both constricted blood vessels and irritated nerves and muscles, all working together to create a severe headache.

What You Need to Know About Referred Pain

Referred pain is pain that is caused by a medical problem in one part of your body that is actually experienced in another part of your body. The cervicogenic headache we discussed earlier is an excellent example of referred pain. Although the problem lies in the neck, upper back, or shoulders, most or all of the pain is experienced as severe pain in the head.

As we also mentioned earlier, often people with such pain don't even notice that their neck or shoulders hurt. It is only when either the doctor physically examines them in these locations and they wince, or the doctor feels the tight muscle (much like you can feel the tightness of the calf muscle when you have a charley horse–type cramp). The pain in their heads is so severe that it overwhelms the pain in the neck or shoulder area; and only direct pressure in the painful area brings the neck or shoulder pain to their attention.

It's important to determine if your problem is caused by referred pain because the source of your pain needs to be accurately determined to effectively alleviate your headaches. If your head hurts and you take a migraine medication, but your actual problem is an arthritic condition in your neck, you usually won't gain much relief from the medication.

When the doctor discovers that you have referred pain, she can treat the arthritic condition, tightened muscles, the other problem in your neck, or wherever the referred pain is located and consequently help you obtain the pain relief that you're longing for.

Now you have evaluated how much your chronic severe headaches are dominating your life, and found out a few things about headache pain. You're ready to read on to the next chapter, where you will begin to explore what kind of headache you really have, to get you on the road to recovery.

CHAPTER 2

What Kind of Headache Do I Have? Figuring Out Your Particular Pain Puzzle

If you believe that one headache is pretty much interchangeable with any other one, including chronic severe headaches, then you're like most people. Unfortunately, you're also wrong, as they are. There are several major types of headaches, and they are very different from each other. While there are some common traits (such as severe head pain) between some of the major types, each one comes with different causes and symptoms.

So, why should you care about what type of headaches you're experiencing? Because when your headaches become chronic and severe, it's important to identify the type of headache you're suffering from so you can better obtain the relief that you need. What works for a migraine generally won't work for a sinus headache and vice versa. Knowing the type of headache you have is an important clue that will lead you and your doctor to hunting down your personal headache cure.

Don't worry that you'll need to amass complex medical knowledge or become a headache expert to gain relief from your pain.

We're here to tell you that is not necessary. Instead, a general idea of what's going on will be extremely useful to you as well as to your doctor. In this chapter we provide a basic overview on the primary types of headaches that most people suffer from. This chapter is also interactive, because we offer you a self-evaluation to take to help you zero in on the type of headaches you're most likely suffering from. After you have taken the self-evaluation and read our analysis of your responses, we advise that you first read the rest of this chapter, "Seeing a Doctor and Getting a Diagnosis" and "Finding a Good Doctor, When Necessary" as well as Chapter 3, "Identifying Your Headache Triggers," which can help you pinpoint possible triggers that could be causing your individual problem. Next, read the specific chapters that we suggest.

A Self-Evaluation: What Could Be Causing *Your* Headaches?

For most people, their chronic headaches fall into a pattern; they are migraines, cervicogenic headaches, tension-type headaches, sinus headaches, rebound headaches, or cluster headaches. Many people also have what is known as a *mixed headache disorder*, which is a combination of headache types. Some people suffer from daily headaches, which is a pretty terrible situation to be in. But no matter what type of headache you have, remember one of our underlying principles discussed in the previous chapter: most often you *can* feel better.

Although it's important to see your doctor to find out what's causing your headaches, you can obtain an idea of some possible causes by responding to our self-evaluation questions and reading the analysis at the end of the section. Answer "yes" or "no" to each question based on how you usually feel.

1. Before my headache pain hits, I see weird patterns before my eyes, like lightning bolts or jagged lines.
2. The pain starts in my neck and later moves to my head.

3. My headaches started (or became more frequent) after I was injured in a car crash.
4. The pain is in my forehead and it is agonizing. It usually lasts no more than several hours and then goes away.
5. My eyes and/or nose are running when my head hurts.
6. Ice on my forehead gives me some relief.
7. When I have a headache, light bothers me a lot, and I need to be in a darkened room.
8. Drinking something caffeinated sometimes makes me feel better, but I still get many headaches.
9. I take headache medicine every day or nearly every day.
10. If I drink milk or consume dairy products, it gives me a headache.
11. I have been diagnosed with anemia as an adult.
12. My teeth really hurt when I get a headache.
13. I have an extremely severe headache, unlike one I've ever had before in my life.
14. When the weather gets wet or hot and humid, my headaches get worse.
15. My headaches are exactly like my mother's headaches.
16. (For women) Every time I get my period, I get a sick headache.

Now let's analyze your responses, one by one, and based on your responses, we'll direct you to the chapters that are the most important for you.

Question 1: I Have Visual Auras Before My Headaches

Many people have heard of the migraine headache, a severe headache that sends most sufferers to their beds for the duration of the pain, until either their medication kicks in or the headache becomes more tolerable.

Migraines are extremely painful headaches that are often accompanied by nausea and vomiting, and many patients also experience nasal congestion and watery eyes. Untreated attacks can last anywhere from four hours to three days. (Yes, you read that right. Some people have migraines that last three *days*. Hopefully, you are not one of them!)

Most "migraineurs," or people with chronic migraines, also have specific sensitivities or "triggers" that are associated with their headaches, that seem to cause their headaches or make them much worse—such as a sensitivity to bright light or loud noise. However, everyone's trigger is different—one migraineur may be sunlight-sensitive while another is prone to developing migraines after eating certain foods.

If you see weird or jagged patterns that aren't really there, and these images occur before the onset of a headache, you're not losing your mind. About 20–30 percent of all migraineurs experience *migraine aura*—which is a sensation that precedes the actual headache—sometimes by an hour or more and at other times by just a few minutes. If you are experiencing this, be sure to tell your doctor about it. An aura could be a tactile sensation, such as numbness and tingling in your face. It could even be a sound, such as a sudden ringing in the ears that goes away when the headache's gone. Many people have visual auras—for example, seeing jagged lines in front of their face that aren't really there.

If you experience auras, they can forewarn you to watch out—a migraine is on the way—giving you time to take preemptive action. Usually you'll need to take medication, and given enough time, you may be able to block the full headache pain—making it more like a glancing blow than a direct hit. Read Chapter 7 on migraines for further information. If the patterns don't go away after the headache starts or when it's over, you should see an ophthalmologist, a medical doctor who specializes in eye diseases.

Question 2: Neck Pain That Becomes Head Pain

If your pain starts in your neck and then seems to travel to your head, you may have a cervicogenic headache. The cervicogenic headache, as discussed earlier, is a headache that is caused by a problem located in your neck, upper spine, or shoulders. However, it feels primarily like a severe headache to you; you may not even *notice* the pain in your neck or shoulders—although some people do. The cervicogenic headache is often misdiagnosed, and thus, this headache pattern will continue on unless or until you're properly diagnosed and treated. If you suffer from frequent, chronic headaches despite various treatment attempts, this may be your problem.

This form of headache could be caused by excessive muscle tension, a spinal disk problem, arthritis, whiplash from a car crash, or several other major causes. These headaches may be triggered by a variety of events, and you can find more information on cervicogenic headaches and what you can do about them in Part II.

Question 3: My Headaches Started After a Car Crash

If you were experiencing few or no headaches and then you were in a car crash and subsequently started suffering from many headaches, these headaches may be directly related to the car crash. You could have a common form of a cervicogenic headache, known as "whiplash." The impact of a car crash can force the head to move violently forward and then back, several times or more. (Did you ever see an ad with crash-test dummies being tossed about? Usually their heads jerk violently forward and back.) Read more about whiplash in Chapter 4 and what to do about it in Chapter 5.

Question 4: Short-Term Forehead Pain

If your headaches are located in your forehead and usually go away after a few hours, even without any medication or treatment, you may be suffering from cluster headaches, although it's also possible it might be a mild sinus attack. Migraine headaches usually occur on one side of the head, rather than centering in the forehead region.

Cluster headaches are very severe headaches that usually last an hour or two, causing pain to the forehead and eyes. Then they're gone. Some patients experience nasal congestion and watery eyes. As mentioned in Chapter 1, males are the primary sufferers of chronic cluster headaches, but females may also suffer from them.

These headaches are very debilitating, but there are good solutions available for chronic sufferers.

Just because they're brief doesn't mean that cluster headaches are any less painful than the other forms of chronic headaches discussed in this book. As doctors, we know that they can be extremely painful. Read Chapter 8 for more information on cluster headaches and what to do about them.

Question 5: Runny Nose and/or Eyes

If your headache pain is accompanied by a runny nose and/or watery eyes, you may be suffering from a sinus headache and/or a sinus infection. The *sinus headache* is a common problem for many people, although recent studies have indicated that patients formerly diagnosed with sinus headaches may actually suffer from migraines instead. With the true sinus headache, the sinus passages in your head become inflamed and often clogged with mucus, and they don't drain properly. Thus, nasal congestion is common. Bacteria may build up and you may develop sinusitis, an inflammation and infection of the sinuses. Appropriate antibiotics should clear up this infection. However, if the infection is viral (or if it's really a migraine or another form of headache), antibiotics won't help. Doctors diagnose sinus headaches with X-rays; but sometimes they skip the X-rays and go solely by the patient's complaints and the location of the pain (usually in the forehead area, especially just above, below, or between the eyes). If your doctor has diagnosed you with frequent bouts of sinusitis without ever taking any X-rays, you may have another headache problem altogether and should consider consulting another physician.

You may also be suffering from a migraine, because many migraineurs look like they have severe colds or the flu—even though their sinuses are just fine when their X-rays are checked by the physician—and patients with cluster headaches may also experience a runny nose and watery eyes. This is precisely why you need to see your doctor to get an accurate diagnosis.

Question 6: Icing the Forehead Helps

If placing ice on your forehead makes you feel better, you may suffer from many different types of headaches, including migraines, cluster headaches, and sinus headaches. It's actually more important to consider if icing does *not* give you any relief. In that case, you're more likely to be suffering from a cervicogenic headache, especially if you also answered "yes" to the second question, on whether neck pain occurs before your headache.

Question 7: Light Sensitivity

Many people with headaches are highly sensitive to intense light, especially people with chronic migraines. If, upon the onset of a severe headache, your first impulse would be to make a beeline for a dark cave rather than moving toward a brightly lit area, you're a clear candidate for migraines. However, other headache sufferers also report an intense sensitivity to light, especially people with cervicogenic headaches. We talk more about light sensitivity and other headache triggers in Chapter 3.

Question 8: Caffeine Makes My Headache Better or Worse

Many people report that consuming something with caffeine helps their headache, which may indicate that they have either cervicogenic headaches or tension-type headaches. A *tension-type headache* is a headache that stems from extremely tight muscles in the head or neck. It may also be a subset of the cervicogenic headache, if your head pain stems from a problem in the upper back, neck, or shoulders. Despite its name, the tension-type headache is not necessarily caused by too much stress in your life. The "tension" in this form of headache refers to overtensed muscles rather than to a stressful experience you may have had. (At the risk of confusing you, however, extreme stress *can* sometimes trigger a tension-type headache in people who are prone to them.) Tension-type headaches are extremely common and they are also treatable, as well as preventable, in most people.

Excessive caffeine can also *cause* headaches. If you're a heavy consumer of caffeinated beverages, your body will develop a need for caffeine. This means if you consume less (or no) caffeine, your brain will rebel with a withdrawal headache, and it can be severe. Tapering off caffeine slowly can help you avoid the withdrawal headache. Caffeine acts on the central nervous system, and most people should consume no more than 250–300 mg of caffeine per day. According to the International Food Information Council Foundation in Washington, D.C., a cup of brewed coffee (6 ounces) has about 100 mg of caffeine, while the same amount of iced tea has 40 mg. An 8-ounce can of a caffeinated soft drink (whether it's diet soda or not) has about 24 mg of caffeine. However, some coffees and soft drinks contain much more caffeine.

For some people, giving up caffeine has abolished their headaches altogether. In a small study of headaches in children and adolescents, published in a 2003 issue of *Cephalgia*, researchers reported on 36 children and adolescents who suffered from daily or near-daily headaches. They were also very heavy cola drinkers. When the subjects were withdrawn from caffeine, 33 of the 36 became headache-free.

Keep in mind that some foods, such as chocolate, also contain a lot of caffeine. An ounce of milk chocolate has about 6 mg of caffeine and an ounce of dark chocolate or semisweet chocolate has about 20 mg. So if you're a chocoholic who doesn't want to give up sweets, at least cut back on your coffee or cola consumption, and choose milk chocolate rather than dark or semisweet chocolate. In addition, it's important to look at the medication you are taking, as some headache medications contain caffeine—such as prescribed Fioricet (butalbital) and some over-the-counter headache remedies.

Question 9: Taking Daily Headache Medicine

If you need to take headache medicine every day, you may have a problem with *rebound headaches*, which are *caused* by headache medicine. Your brain never quite normalizes to the no-pain state, and if you don't take the headache medicine, the headache pain can become excruciating. It seems really unfair, but sometimes the medications that you take to *prevent* headaches can actually *induce* more headaches as a side effect of taking the drug, often perpetuating a vicious headache cycle. If you are taking a headache medication on a daily or frequent basis (three or more days per week), and have developed chronic headaches, your medication may be the reason for your headaches, and you should consult with your physician about this possibility as he can advise you on the best way to taper off headache medication. In addition, read Chapter 9 for more information on this common type of headache.

Question 10: Some Foods (Like Dairy Products) Give Me a Headache

In addition to foods with caffeine, many people are sensitive to other foods that may trigger a headache. They're usually not allergic to the foods, in the sense that the body creates histamines in direct response to exposure to them, as with people who are allergic to penicillin or bee sting venom. Lactose intolerance is one example of a food sensitivity. Some people's bodies lack the ability to make an enzyme (*lactase*) that enables them to digest dairy products. This means if they consume items like milk, they develop symptoms, and the most common symptom is a severe headache. If you suspect that you may be lactose-intolerant, one simple way to check out your theory is to avoid eating dairy products for a week or so and see if your headaches go away. Your doctor can also run medical tests to find out if you're lactose-intolerant. Read more about foods that act as headache triggers in Chapter 3.

Question 11: I've Had Anemia Before

If you've been diagnosed with anemia before as an adult, based on your blood test results and information that your doctor provided you, it's possible that you may have anemia again. Ask your doctor to check your blood, because anemia can cause severe chronic headaches. Treatment will usually alleviate these headaches. Read more about anemia and other health problems that can trigger severe headaches in Chapter 9.

Question 12: My Teeth Hurt

Dental pain is a valuable diagnostic clue for your physician, so be sure to tell her about it. You may be suffering from a sinus headache. See your dentist in addition to your doctor, to rule out the presence of cavities or dental or sinus infections. When one or several of your teeth hurt, the problem could be a sinus that is draining directly into the nerve of your tooth. You could also have an abscessed tooth and may need a root canal. Simple dental X-rays will usually show the dentist if this is your problem.

Your dentist may also be able to tell if you have a problem with *temporamandibular joint (TMJ) disorder*, since many dentists receive training in diagnosing and treating this condition. If you have TMJ, you may grind your teeth while you're asleep at night (*bruxism*), which further aggravates your headaches. A simple mouth guard that's worn at night and prevents teeth grinding may alleviate minor TMJ problems and resolve your headache situation. Read more about TMJ in Chapter 9.

Question 13: My Headache Is the Worst Pain of My Life

Some headaches are what doctors call *emergency headaches*, because they may be a warning of an impending severe medical problem, such as a stroke or a burst blood vessel (aneurysm) in the brain. Even if you have chronic severe headaches, pay attention if a new headache is very unlike your "normal" headaches and far more severe than usual. If so, get emergency help because time is of the essence. Read more about emergency headaches in Chapter 8 so you're prepared ahead of time, just in case.

Question 14: Wet or Humid Weather Makes My Headaches Start (or Worsen)

Many people are weather-sensitive, and certain types of weather changes may trigger a headache in some people or make a headache that they already have so much worse. Some studies, such as one reported in *Headache* in 2004, have shown that rain and hot, humid weather bothers many headache-prone people a great deal.

We talk more about weather and other headache triggers in Chapter 3.

Question 15: My Headaches Are Exactly Like My Mother's Headaches

This is an important clue to physicians, as a family history of similar headaches, particularly "sick" headaches, is very consistent with a migraine headache. Usually there is a strong genetic component to migraine headaches. We talk more about hereditary migraines and their treatments in Chapter 7.

Question 16: Every Time I Get My Period, I Get a Sick Headache

If you are a woman who gets a headache with your periods, this again relates to the fact that there is a significantly higher female-to-male ratio of migraine headache sufferers. And it's an important point because many women do not make the connection of suffering with a headache during their menstrual cycle. But this unique set of menstrual migraines, also known as *catamenial migraines*, can be quite effectively treated and is discussed further in Chapter 7.

But What If It's a Combination or Other Type of Headache?

Not all headaches fall into a strict migraine, tension-type headache, *or* other headache pattern. Patients may have a *combination headache*—with some of the elements of two or more different types of headache—which can make it a challenging problem for their physicians to diagnose and treat. (And even less fun to experience firsthand!) Often a patient may start out with just one type of headache but over time and owing to various medical interventions may develop a second or third type of headache. We cover these combination headaches in Chapter 8. Experienced physicians can help you with this problem.

In addition, there are many reasons why people develop head-aches, and not all headaches fit into a neat pattern of migraine, cluster headache, another headache type, or even a combination headache. There could be a medical problem that's causing your pain. For example, metabolic problems, such as thyroid disease or diabetes, can sometimes cause chronic headaches, as can systemic problems, such as anemia. Low or high blood pressure can also lead to chronic headaches. In addition, chronic infections can lead to severe headaches, such as sinusitis or infection caused by Lyme disease. Read more about headaches caused by underlying med-ical problems in Chapter 9.

Seeing a Doctor and Getting a Diagnosis

If you are suffering from headaches on a *daily or near-daily basis* (at least three or four times a week), it's very important to see your physician, or if that hasn't helped, to see a new doctor. You may think you *know* that you suffer from migraines, cluster headaches, cervicogenic headaches, or some other form of headache, but let's face it: it's really up to your doctor to make the definitive diag-nosis. And it helps to know how your doctor decides what kind of headache you have. The rest of this chapter is about how physi-cians evaluate your chronic severe headaches. (Or how they *should!*) We also talk about how to find a good physician. Many readers with chronic headaches have given up on their doctors, while others have relocated to a new area and need to find a good headache doc. Read our helpful hints if you're in one of these situations.

Tests Your Doctor May Order

Because chronic headaches may be caused by another illness that you didn't even know you had, most physicians will order labora-tory tests and may also order imaging tests as well. Laboratory tests will help doctors rule out metabolic problems, blood diseases, and infections—all of which can cause severe headaches. For example, if you have iron deficiency anemia and that's the illness causing your headaches, treatment should decrease or altogether eliminate your chronic headache problem. If you have a bacterial infection, then you need antibiotics, and they should help resolve your headaches. If you have a metabolic disorder (like diabetes or thyroid disease) or especially if you have high blood pressure, you need to treat that problem in order to obtain headache relief. Of course, all your tests may come back normal, and then the doctor will consider other possible causes of your severe headaches.

Your physician may also order one or more imaging tests, such as X-rays, a computerized tomography (CT) scan, or a magnetic resonance imaging (MRI) scan. These tests can reveal if there are serious abnormalities or other medical problems that could be causing your headaches.

Laboratory Tests

Most doctors will order a complete blood count (CBC) to rule out anemia and other blood diseases, as well as infections. If the doctor suspects ahead of time that you may have an iron deficiency, he'll also order a check of your iron blood levels. The doctor may also order a test of your levels of vitamins and minerals, to check if you have any deficiencies. In addition, the doctor will usually order a *thyroid-stimulating hormone (TSH)* blood test, to determine whether your thyroid blood level is in the normal range, or if it's hypothyroid (underactive) or hyperthyroid (overactive). If the test reveals you are deficient in thyroid hormone, it's easy enough to take thyroid supplements. If you're hyperthyroid, you'll need a treatment plan.

Your doctor may also order a test of your sodium levels. *Hyponatremia* (below-normal levels of sodium in the blood) can cause severe headaches. Sometimes people with hypothyroidism develop hyponatremia, so you may have both problems— although it's possible to have low sodium levels and normal thyroid levels, or normal sodium levels and abnormal thyroid levels.

The doctor should also test your blood glucose levels. *Hypoglycemia* (below-normal blood sugar) can cause extreme headaches, and this problem can develop into a medical emergency if the glucose level dips too low. The test will also reveal if you have diabetes, which is usually a problem of hyperglycemia, or blood sugar levels that are too high. However, people with diabetes sometimes experience hypoglycemia as their blood sugar levels go up and down. Chronic hypoglycemia needs to be treated because it can be very dangerous, especially for people with diabetes. (In the worst case, it can cause coma and even death.)

It is also common for doctors to run tests looking to see if there is an inflammatory process at work in your body. A simple *erythrocyte sedimentation rate (ESR)* test will quickly determine this. If the ESR is positive, your doctor may follow up with additional tests, since the sedimentation rate is not specific for any one type of inflammation.

If there is any concern that you may have been exposed to toxins, unique chemicals, or drugs, your doctor may check a urine drug screen. This test can screen for many common drugs of abuse but also screens for many less commonly suspected toxins. A 24-hour urine screen for drugs and heavy metals/toxins can also be used to follow up on a screening test.

A simple blood test for vitamin B_{12} may also be checked, as this is a very important vitamin for the nervous system. Low levels of B_{12} can not only lead to headaches but can also lead to confusion, muscle problems and cramping, and numbness and tingling throughout the body.

X-Rays and Imaging Tests

Your doctor may request X-rays or imaging tests before he sees you, although often such tests are ordered after your physical examination. X-rays can show minor or major fractures, while a CT scan or an MRI are better at identifying serious illnesses in the brain, such as a tumor or an aneurysm (burst blood vessel in the brain). Even though most people with chronic headaches have normal CTs and MRIs, doctors use them to rule out serious problems. In addition, any time there is a significant change in the frequency and severity of your headaches, it's a good idea to have an imaging study of the brain to rule out any very serious problems.

These imaging studies can also reveal arthritis, cervical disk problems (disks are the pads between the bones in your neck and spine), or other problems that need treatment. Some of these problems may be directly causing your headaches, especially if you suffer from cervicogenic headaches.

The Physical Examination

Your doctor needs to look you in the face (and the head, the neck, and the rest of you) before he can really diagnose you. The laboratory work and X-rays or imaging tests will provide important information to your physician, but sometimes what is most needed is for you to show the doctor where you hurt, so he can examine the muscles and tissues in that area and see if there's anything that's apparently wrong.

Before You See the Doctor

Usually, if it's your first appointment with the physician, you'll need to fill out a form about your medical history. You'll respond to whether you've been diagnosed with a variety of illnesses, as well as describe past surgeries you've had and the medications that you currently take. Don't forget to list any supplements you take, such as St. John's wort, feverfew, or vitamin C. Take the time to read every question and answer them all honestly. This is important information for your doctor! In addition, before you see the doctor, it's also a good idea to jot down the two or three most important questions or issues you want to discuss. It's easy to forget them during your examination, when you're distracted by what's going on in the office or by what the doctor says. The topics that you jot down may also be covered in the medical history form you fill out, but sometimes they aren't, so it's best to write down your primary concerns.

Jane, 35, one of our patients, wanted to tell us that she wondered if her severe daily headaches might have something to do with a fall she took the month before, when she slightly hit her head. She considered it a minor fall that caused a glancing blow, but decided she should tell us anyway. (She was right.) Jane also wondered if the minor fender-bender accident she was in recently, in which she had forgotten to wear her seat belt, could have anything to do with these new headaches.

Jane wrote her list:

1. *Fall in October—headaches afterward*
2. *Minor car accident in November—no seat belt. Headaches afterward*

Jane didn't worry about us yelling at her for not wearing her seat belt because she knew she should have worn it and even reassured us that she always buckles up now.

It's important to be as candid as Jane was with your own doctor even if your behavior may sometimes be problematic, such as you've been advised to give up smoking or drinking and you really haven't. Don't lie and say you have. The doctor needs good information so he can give you the best care.

In most cases, you'll see the nurse before you see your physician. One simple important test administered by the nurse is the blood pressure test. If you have a problem with your blood pressure, it can lead to severe chronic headaches. If you have hypertension, or above-normal blood pressure, it may be high because of another illness you have, *or* chronic hypertension could be *the* illness that's making you so headache-prone. If you have hypotension, or below-normal blood pressure, it can also lead to extreme headache pain, and it, too, needs to be further investigated.

During the Exam

After you see the nurse and she writes down the numbers of your blood pressure, pulse, and (maybe) your body temperature, the next step is to see your physician. In most cases, the doctor will first ask you what your primary problem is, how long you've had it, and if you know of anything that seems to make the problem better or worse. Now is the time to bring out your short list of questions, such as the one Jane made.

If the doctor examines you by pressing somewhere that hurts, make sure to let him know. Jane flinched when we pressed an area on her neck that was really painful, and when we asked her if it hurt, she said it certainly did! Remember, you don't get extra points for bravery if you conceal your pain. Instead, by doing so, you make it harder for the physician to pinpoint your pain, and you're actually working against yourself. It's important to understand that you and your physician are partners, so the better you work together, the better you can feel.

Zeroing in on Your Underlying Problem

Good doctors consider your symptoms (what you complain about), your signs or indicators of disease (such as fever or a rapid pulse), your medical history, the results of your lab and imaging studies, and the physical examination results in order to come up with a diagnosis. Most doctors perform a *differential diagnosis*, which means that they consider the broad spectrum of medical problems that you might have. The physician rules out many conditions until homing in on the most likely culprit for your headache pain.

For example, with Jane, we ordered an MRI of her head and neck to make sure the fall and/or the car accident didn't cause any minor fractures. The MRI was negative for fractures but did show that Jane had arthritis in her neck, as well as some swelling of the disks in the cervical spine, a condition that is known as *degenerative disk disease*. We noted that Jane had pain when we lightly pressed in her cervical spine area. Jane's lab tests came back with all normal results, so she didn't have an infection or a metabolic disorder. Her blood pressure was normal, so she didn't have hypertension. Going by our experience and the information we'd compiled, we considered the type of headache that she might have. All the information led us to believe that Jane's chronic headaches were cervicogenic headaches and from that diagnosis we made a treatment plan for her.

Finding a Good Doctor, When Necessary

Your current physician may be fine, so don't assume we think everyone needs a new doctor. We don't! However, if you are unhappy with your physician and/or he has not referred you to a headache specialist, such as a neurologist, it may be time for you to find a new doctor. You may also need a new doctor because you've relocated to a different area, or maybe a doctor you really liked has retired. This section offers basic tips on what to look for in a headache doc. But first, let's talk about the difference between generalist doctors who treat chronic headaches and neurologists.

Your Family Physician

For many patients, family practitioners and generalist internists who routinely treat chronic headaches can provide an adequate diagnosis and treatment. In fact, some internists and family practitioners are very adept at diagnosing and treating chronic severe headaches. However, keep in mind that the nonspecialist treats many different types of illnesses, and consequently, it's often difficult for him to stay on top of the latest breakthroughs in headache research or know about the newest headache medications or treatments.

If you're not obtaining good results in resolving your headache problem and need a new physician, seek out an internist with a special interest in headaches. Or see a neurologist, a physician trained in problems of the brain and spinal cord.

If another physician was treating your headaches (and you need a change in doctors), ask your primary care doctor for a recommendation. Even if she recommended the specialist you currently have and don't like, she's very likely to know more than one headache expert. If you don't have a primary care doctor, ask your other doctors for referrals; or ask your dentist, pharmacist, and others involved in health care if they know of a doctor who likes treating headaches. (Many doctors hate treating headaches, thinking they're boring or annoying problems. You don't want one of them treating you.)

You could also ask your friends and family members who live in your geographic area if they have or had chronic headaches (headaches on 15 or more days each month); and if they do, consult the physician who has helped them.

Going to a Neurologist

We're neurologists, so we are biased in thinking that neurologists are best at treating headaches. As with finding a good internist, the best way to locate a good neurologist is to ask your primary care physician who he would take a family member to see, if that person suffered from constant headaches. But don't stop there. Also ask your friends and family, as well as others in the medical profession, for their recommendations.

Questions to Ask Your Prospective Physician

Whether you decide to use an internist, family practitioner, or a neurologist to help you with your chronic headaches, when you're considering a new physician, you should seek answers to questions that help you know about the doctor's experience with treating chronic headaches and how the doctor feels about headache patients.

If possible, talk to the prospective doctor on the telephone yourself, or send him an e-mail. (If the doctor has a website, his e-mail address might be available there. Check for a "contact us" box on the site; it may connect you to the doctor's e-mail address.) *Note:* Once you find your doctor, don't use the e-mail as a way of constantly contacting the doctor. Make appointments.

Do *not* ask your questions of the person who answers the phone. Receptionists rarely are aware of the doctor's beliefs and policies and are almost invariably the wrong people to talk to. It would be like asking a bank teller for complicated advice on how to refinance your home. You need to speak to someone in authority who knows something. It may not be the equivalent of the bank president (or the doctor you want to talk to) but it is probably a loan officer who knows what you need to know (or the doctor's nurse or physician's assistant).

When you call, ask if you can have a brief conversation with the doctor at his convenience, and if so, when would be the best time to call (because you're looking for a new doctor). You may not be able to talk to a very busy doctor, but sometimes the answer is yes. If the doctor can't be reached, ask to speak to the doctor's assistant or nurse. This person should know the answers to all (or most) of your questions. In addition, never ask the receptionist or any employee of the doctor if he's a good doctor. What do you expect them to say? They work for him and probably want to keep their jobs. Use common sense and think how you would feel if you were working for the doctor and someone asked you one of your questions. If your question still seems okay and would help you in screening the doctor, then go ahead and ask it.

Sometimes you need to make an appointment to see a doctor before you have an opportunity to ask your questions. If this happens, it's still definitely worth making a copayment or even paying an entire fee to do so. It's better to screen your doctor in (or out) on the first visit than to see her many times and get nowhere.

We've included some questions to consider asking your prospective physician (or the nurse or physician's assistant, if need be). You can add more questions to this list, but keep the list short.

1. **How many headache patients have you (or the doctor) treated?** The doctor should have treated at least 50–100 headache patients, so that he has the experience that you need.
2. **Are headaches a major problem for your patients?** Try to get this answer directly from the doctor and listen closely to the answer. If the doctor says yes, and they're all a bunch of whiners, then he's not the physician for you. He is not interested in treating headache patients.
3. **Do many of your patients with headaches need triptan medications?** If the doctor doesn't know what

you're talking about, this is a negative indication. *Triptans* are migraine medications and even if migraines *aren't your problem*, they are common enough that most doctors who treat headaches should know about them.

4. **Are you on my insurance company's list of preferred providers?** Insurance companies generally check out doctors first and will not recommend someone who has a spotty record and been sued a lot. However, it's also true that a very good doctor may not be on some insurance company's list, for many reasons. Don't assume someone is a bad doctor just because he or she isn't on a list of preferred providers.

5. **Can you cure me?** When you first meet a doctor, most will respond to this question by saying that they don't know, but they'll try to help you. If the doctor asserts right away that he *can* cure you, before you've had any laboratory tests or a physical examination, be very skeptical of this doctor.

6. **Have you done any special work or research in the area of headache pain?** Not all doctors have done headache research, but if your doctor is truly interested in headaches, a "yes" may be very reassuring.

7. **What is the doctor's policy when a headache becomes a crisis?** Will he send you to the hospital emergency room or does either he or an associate have the ability to see you within 24 hours to reevaluate your condition? If the doctor has the capability to see you or have an associate see you, this is a positive indication.

In this chapter, we offered you a self-evaluation to help you zero in on the type of headaches you're most likely to be suffering from, covering the basic types of headaches and how doctors diagnose them. In the next chapter, we describe the primary headache triggers. It's a don't-miss chapter.

CHAPTER 3

Identifying Your Headache Triggers

Anne, 22, came to us complaining of extremely severe headaches. After a thorough medical history and examination, we talked to Anne about possible triggers for her headaches. We eventually discovered that every time Anne purchased a chocolate candy bar from the office vending machine, she was hit with a splitting headache within an hour. One didn't need to be Sherlock Holmes to realize that chocolate might be a headache trigger for her—but we tested our theory by having Anne refrain from all candy bars for a week. And guess what? No headaches!

Chocolate is *not* a headache trigger for everyone. However, most people, like Anne, who have chronic severe headaches also have particular items or events that frequently induce their headaches. For some individuals, bright sunlight or loud noises are their primary headache triggers, while for others, it's certain foods or types of foods that propel them into a painful headache. Still, for others, the main headache trigger may be certain smells, such as heavy perfume, gasoline, or tobacco smoke. It can even be a type of weather that brings on their headaches, such as the onset of a rainy or snowy day. Many women suffer from hormonal headaches—headaches that occur before or during their periods, when they take birth control pills, or even when they take hormone

Triggers and Headache Types

Sometimes your headache triggers depend on the *type* of headaches that you suffer from; for example, some studies, such as one reported in *Headache* in 1999, indicate that people with chronic migraines are particularly prone to develop headaches from exposure to bright light, while those with cervicogenic headaches are more acutely sensitive to loud noise. A further problem is that if you're sensitive to certain items or events in a nonheadache state, these triggers will often bother you even more intensely when you are actively suffering from a headache. Consequently, if bright light causes you discomfort most of the time, then when you get a headache, intense light will *really* bother you. (Although for some people, bright light is only a problem when they have a headache.)

In a study published in a 1999 issue of *Headache*, researchers studied the sensitivity to physical stimuli among people with chronic headaches, including 68 migraine patients, 45 patients with tension-type headaches, 46 with cluster headaches, 23 patients with cervicogenic headaches, and 71 control subjects who didn't experience chronic headaches (who were included in the study for a basis of comparison).

When they didn't have headaches, people with migraines felt the most discomfort from bright light. Only 1 percent of the control group was severely discomforted by intense light, compared to 27 percent of the migraineurs. The situation worsened with a headache. When they had a headache and were also exposed to intense light, 68 percent of the subjects with migraines had severe discomfort.

Interestingly, extreme light also affected people with other forms of headaches. For example, in the nonheadache state, some

replacement therapy during menopause. Severe stress is also a powerful trigger for numerous people. Many people have more than one trigger, so you may be sensitive to weather changes, *and* some foods, *and* loud noise, and so forth. The problem is even worse if your particular triggers don't cause a headache every sin-

people with cervicogenic headaches were greatly bothered by extreme light (13 percent), and among people with cluster headaches, 7 percent were bothered. Once they *had* headaches, bright light really caused discomfort to people with cluster headaches (57 percent), cervicogenic headaches (44 percent), and tension-type headaches (31 percent).

In addition, the researchers found that excessive noise significantly discomforted many people with headaches. Severe noise bothered 3 percent of the control group—compared to the 17 percent with chronic cervicogenic headaches, 9 percent with chronic migraines, and 7 percent each with tension-type headaches and cluster headaches—all of whom found loud noise extremely bothersome in a nonheadache state.

Once they actually had a headache, however, people with migraines felt the worst from severe noise (62 percent), although individuals with other forms of headache also suffered, including those with cervicogenic headaches (52 percent), cluster headaches (44 percent), and tension-type headaches (36 percent).

The researchers also noted that 46 percent of the migraineurs were sensitive to smells, compared to the 13 to 17 percent of individuals with other headache types.

They also found that driving a car often provoked a headache in patients with cervicogenic headaches (61 percent) and migraines (50 percent), but once they had a headache, 79 percent of the migraineurs and 78 percent of the cervicogenic headache subjects felt severe discomfort from driving a car.

gle time. It's a little like Russian roulette; sometimes that chocolate bar will bring on a migraine and sometimes it won't.

Sometimes it's the *lack* of something that causes headaches, such as a lack of food or a lack of sleep. You skip lunch and a headache starts up. Or you don't get your nightly Z's and so trigger a headache. If you do this often enough, you can develop chronic headaches.

The good news is that once you become aware of what your headache triggers are, you can become proactive in reducing their impact on you. For example, depending on your triggers, you can avoid foods that induce headaches, or limit your exposure to direct sunlight or intense light. Even if a trigger is something you can't physically change, such as the weather, you can still be aware of the weather forecast, and, when needed, take preventive medication or other actions that your doctor recommends. Knowledge really is power!

But maybe you're not sure what your headache triggers are. If so, you're like most people with chronic severe headaches. They may know one or two things that seem to set them off, but they're oblivious to other triggers that are major problems for them. As you read this chapter, note whether one or more of the headache triggers we discuss seems to cause a problem for you.

Analyzing the When and Where of Your Headaches: A Self-Evaluation

What about you? What are the things that trigger *your* headaches? Take our self-test and answer "yes" or "no" to the following questions about possible headache triggers. Then read our analysis of your responses and what lifestyle or environmental changes you may be able to make in order to prevent your headaches from coming on or getting worse.

1. Weather changes seem to make my headaches start or get worse.
2. If I eat cheddar cheese, or other types of foods or drinks, I get a headache.
3. If I skip a meal (or two), I get a headache.
4. If I don't get 7–8 hours of sleep, I'm likely to develop a headache.

5. Working on my computer or going online for many hours causes my headaches.
6. Bright lights or intense sunlight gives me a headache.
7. Loud noises can lead to my headaches.
8. If I get really stressed-out, I get a headache.
9. For women: I get more headaches before or during my period.
10. I've started taking a new medication, and my headaches have gotten worse.
11. I take aspirin or Tylenol every day.
12. I'm a smoker.
13. I exercise strenuously every day or almost every day.
14. Some odors really bother me.

Question 1: Weather Changes: Yes, Changes in Weather *Can* Cause Headaches

It's true. Precipitation (rain or snow) can precipitate a headache. Many people have believed that their headaches were directly affected by the weather, and their doctors scoffed. But not any-more, because studies *have* shown weather changes really can induce headaches. The most recent study was published in a 2004 issue of *Headache*, based on 77 patients with chronic migraines. The researchers found that more than half (51 percent) of the patients were sensitive to weather conditions, which led to severe headaches. There were no gender differences, as both men and women reported weather sensitivities.

The greatest number of patients who were weather-sensitive reacted to low barometric pressure. The next group of patients who reacted the most to weather changes responded to falling pressure. A third group developed headaches with any change in air pressure. In contrast, few people specifically reacted to either a high barometric pressure or to a rising barometric pressure.

What do low and high barometric pressure mean? It's a mea-sure of air pressure, and the standard sea-level barometric pressure is 29.92 inches of mercury. When pressure rises, it goes above this level to about 30 or 31. This pressure level indicates sunny and dry weather. If the pressure starts to fall below 29.92 to around 29, it means that rain or snow is probably on its way; and if it falls further to around 28, it means severe storm conditions are coming, such as a hurricane.

What does this mean for you? Obviously you can't change the weather to suit you. (Although it does sound like an appealing idea!) One thing you *can* do is find out whether you are weather-sensitive. You may need to purchase a barometer, so you can track when the atmospheric pressure is low or falling, if these conditions are headache triggers for you. Or you can check out the Weather Channel on television. In fact, if you have access to the Internet, you can go to a Weather Channel website at weather .com/activities/health/achesandpains and type in your zip code to find out if the air pressure will be staying about the same, or rising or falling tomorrow in your area. (We typed in a zip code in Yonkers, New York, and found out that the air pressure was 30.35 and falling, and a snowstorm was expected the next day. Conditions in Yonkers were clear and dry, but would soon be migraine-making weather for some weather-sensitive headache sufferers.)

The Weather Channel website also includes an "aches and pains" index that takes into account air pressure, humidity, wind, and other factors and comes up with an index for people who are prone to headaches or arthritis pain from weather changes. An index of 9 or 10 means watch out if you're weather-sensitive.

You can use our headache trigger chart at the end of this chapter, or make your own chart to help you track whether the weather changes may be a headache trigger for you.

If you find that you are very sensitive to a falling barometer, headache-wise, you can take preventive medication ahead of time. (We cover these types of medications in more detail in Chapter 10.) If you're sensitive to bright sunshine, wear sunglasses outside to limit your exposure and limit your time on the beach. If high humidity bothers you, you may wish to buy a dehumidifier for your home or workplace. There are solutions for every headache trigger.

Question 2: Potential Food Triggers

Food is a headache trigger in about half of people with migraines and 20–30 percent of patients with other types of headaches. For some people, frequent culprits that launch a headache include: aged cheese; salty foods; or foods that contain tannin, such as avocados, dark beer, and nuts. Some people find that wines with a high concentration of tannin (frequently found in a lot of red wines) or any form of alcohol induces a headache. (We're not talking about drinking to excess, which causes another form of headache, commonly called the "hangover.") For some people, even one glass of red wine is enough to send them into Migraine Land. However, everyone is different, and you may be able to load up on cheddar while a tiny portion of something with nuts in it induces a major headache.

Other common headache triggers are foods with additives, such as aspartame (used to sweeten food, such as diet foods and drinks) or monosodium glutamate (MSG), a flavor enhancer. Foods with nitrates, such as hot dogs, ham, pepperoni, and bologna, can also be headache triggers to some people. In the past, Chinese restaurants loaded up their foods with MSG, so if you ate Chinese food and subsequently developed a severe headache, it might have been an MSG problem. (Now many Chinese restaurants avoid using MSG, and you can also ask the waiter to make sure that the chef refrains from using it in your food.) Additionally, there are many prepared foods that contain MSG, so don't think that as long as you never eat out, you'll be fine. There may be more MSG in your powdered soup mix than you'd ever find in a restaurant entrée. Read the labels on the foods that you buy in the supermarket. If MSG is a headache trigger for you, and it is a prominent ingredient in the food you are purchasing (the ingredients are listed in order of their prominence), simply don't buy this food.

As wonderful as newly baked bread smells, fresh bread is also a headache trigger for some individuals, according to experts at the American Council for Headache Education. Also, some individuals are sensitive to carbohydrates; and with the excitement of "low-carb diets," many headache sufferers who go on such diets have found that their headaches have improved drastically. Even fruits can induce headaches in some individuals, especially citrus fruits, while other people are hypersensitive to highly spiced foods.

Researchers disagree on whether chocolate can trigger headaches. For example, some experts believe if a woman develops more headaches when she eats chocolate, it's more likely to be stress or hormones that is the underlying problem, rather than the chocolate itself. The theory is that stressed-out women or women bothered by hormonal changes are more likely to crave and eat chocolate. However, whether you're a woman or a man, if you consider yourself a chocoholic, it's a good idea to track whether you develop headaches within 12 hours or so of consuming something chocolate. If so, chocolate may be a trigger for you. The 12-hour rule applies to other foods as well. If you're going to get a headache from food, it'll happen sometime within 12 hours.

As discussed earlier in Chapter 2, caffeinated drinks or foods can cause headaches in some people, and chocolate contains caffeine, as does coffee, tea, and many carbonated soft drinks. Paying attention to when your headaches occur and what you ate before the onset of a headache can help you determine if you have food triggers, so that you can avoid them. Start using our suggested headache-trigger diary at the end of this chapter to help you determine what your trigger foods might be.

Question 3: Failing to Eat Regular Meals

You don't have to follow a government plan of so many helpings of vegetables, fruits, meats, and so on each and every day, but you should eat something during the daytime, about every 4–5 hours or so. Skipping meals is a common headache trigger, especially among women. If you don't eat at regular intervals during the day, your blood sugar level will fall. Some individuals become hypoglycemic or close to hypoglycemic, and hypoglycemia induces a very bad headache. It's not just what your sugar level is, but it's also how quickly it shifts. So if you are sensitive to blood sugar changes, eating at regular intervals is a must. Even a little snack can sometimes help you feel better; however, try to avoid high-calorie snacks, at least most of the time.

Question 4: Sleepless Nights and Sleep Disorders

It's not only children who need a good night's sleep. Every adult should sleep about seven hours per night to help the body recover from the day's stressors. If you shortchange your body with a lack of sleep and assume that, for example, because you're 35 years old (or older) and in good health you can get by on five hours a night (or less), you're making a serious mistake. Because you feel so tired, you're likely to cause a headache that may deter you from achieving your goals for the day. Please note that, contrary to popular opinion, sleep is not a time-waster. Let your body have the rest it needs.

Additionally, there's another sleep-related problem that's linked to headaches, called *obstructive sleep apnea,* an illness that causes a person to stop breathing for short periods during sleep. While most people think that sleep apnea is no more than obtrusive snoring, it's a serious health problem. In one study, reported in *Archives of Internal Medicine* in 1999, the researchers found a significant link between headaches and the presence of sleep apnea. The patients most likely to have sleep apnea were those who woke up with a severe headache in the morning. The patients who received treatment for their sleep apnea experienced a dramatic improvement in their headaches.

How do you know if you have sleep apnea? Only your doctor can diagnose this problem, but if you snore loudly (ask your spouse or other family members about this) and are overweight or obese, you're at risk for sleep apnea and should consult with your doctor.

Question 5: Staring at Your Computer Screen for Hours

Most physicians agree that you should not perform tasks on your computer for hours on end, although many of us do this anyway. People tend to hunch over when using their computer, which can cause neck pain and cervicogenic headaches.

The glare of the screen and the infrequent eye blinking that often occurs when people use their computers (blinking about 3–5 times less than normal) can also lead to eye strain, blurred vision, and headaches. This condition is known as *computer vision syndrome* (*CVS*). It's more common among people using computers than among television watchers for several reasons, including that you're a lot closer to your computer monitor when you use it than you are to your television screen while watching your favorite program. In addition, you are probably more intensely engaged in what you're doing when working on the computer than when you're watching a rerun of an old sitcom.

If you must use your computer for an extended period, make sure you don't have your screen set to a blinding white glare. Make adjustments to your computer monitor and choose a light gray or pale shade for the background. (And check the lighting in your room. Many people who use computers are exposed to bright lights, another major headache trigger.) Take a break from the computer, at least for five minutes every hour. Get in the habit of blinking more frequently when you're using the computer. Eye lubricants may also help, but if your eyes are really bothering you, see an ophthalmologist (a doctor who specializes in eye problems). Consider purchasing a flat-screen monitor to cut down on the glare. Taking these actions should help you to significantly cut back on your headaches and their intensity!

Question 6: Shedding Some Light on Your Lighting

As mentioned earlier, bright light is a headache trigger for many people. Many people with chronic migraines wear sunglasses most of the time, even inside buildings. Fluorescent light is a particular trigger for many people who suffer from chronic headaches, especially those with migraines. Some people take their own incandescent lamps off to work with them, and they turn off the fluorescent lights in the room. Some even resort to hiding the "on" and "off" switch for the fluorescent lights by piling up boxes or other objects in front of it. Newer fluorescent lights are much less likely to cause headaches, but according to a *Wall Street Journal* article in 2004, some experts estimate that at least half of all offices still have the same old bad fluorescent lights.

If you think fluorescent light might be a problem for you at work and is triggering your severe chronic headaches, tell your boss. You can also request a work accommodation of changing the lighting so you can avoid headaches, under the Americans with Disabilities Act. It's a good idea to also tell your boss that some researchers have found that natural light improves worker productivity—a nice incentive to give your boss so you can obtain what you need and she has a reason to justify the change to *her* supervisors. (A solution with a benefit to the company is always more readily accepted than a mere complaint.)

What if you work in a windowless office and natural light is out of the question? Poor you! One solution is to ask the boss to upgrade to the newer fluorescent lights, which are less headache-inducing. You could also consider turning off the lights that are directly over your work station.

Question 7: When Loud Noises Lead to Pounding Headaches

You may feel like the pounding in the office next to you is directly transmitted to your brain, in the form of a pounding headache. And you may be right. As discussed earlier in the chapter, loud noise is a key headache trigger for many people. Some people wear earplugs or earmuffs to block out the blaring noise, or they block it with white-noise generators or music. Of course, the best solution is to stay away from loud noise, whenever possible. This generally means that you'll need to avoid earsplitting rock concerts. Sorry! Buy the CD later and listen to it at a normal volume in your home.

What if you can't avoid the noise, because it's your screaming baby perhaps suffering with colic? Try to get some help, and take medications as needed. And remember, your baby will eventually get older.

Question 8: Stress and Headaches

Severe trauma or chronic extreme stress can trigger headaches in some people. In Chapter 1, we talked about the myth that a hectic society causes headaches, which isn't true or everyone would have headaches, since we live in a society that is overall pretty hectic. However, many people *are* prone to react to excessive stress by developing severe headaches. The underlying cause may be that they fail to eat, drink, and/or sleep sufficiently, or it could be the stress alone that makes them headache-prone. In a study reported in a 2003 issue of *Cephalgia*, researchers studied 141 subjects with migraine and 109 controls without migraine. They found that the stress and anxiety levels were significantly higher in the migraine group.

The researchers stated that, "Stress is a primordial factor in the triggering and perpetuation of migraine attacks. The high score of the items 'morning fatigue,' 'intrusive thoughts about work,' 'feeling under pressure,' 'impatience,' and 'irritability' of the stress questionnaire in the migraineurs is particularly significant in the intensive stress response."

Question 9: Hormonal Headaches

Many women get headaches, especially migraines, that are associated with hormonal changes, such as the onset of their monthly period. More women get headaches before their periods than during them. This may be due to a decreasing level of estrogen that occurs before the onset of menstruation.

Some women develop headaches when they take oral contraceptives (because of the hormones in them). Other women who are menopausal get headaches when they use hormone replacement therapy.

In one study of 504 women who suffered from migraines, reported in a 2004 issue of *Headache*, the researchers found that 69 percent of the subjects also had premenstrual syndrome, while 29 percent had menopausal symptoms. Birth control pills or hormone replacement therapy were headache triggers for 64 percent of the group.

If you discover that you are prone to hormonal headaches, there are a variety of solutions, such as taking preventive medication, asking the doctor to change your dosage, and other actions to consider taking. Find out more about menstrual migraines in Chapter 7.

Question 10: Medication-Induced Headaches

Many medications increase the risk of developing headaches, as a side effect of using the drug. Some medications are particularly prone to inducing headaches as a side effect, such as antiulcer medications, high blood pressure medications, oral contraceptives, hormone replacement therapy, and nitroglycerin for heart disease.

If you've started taking a new medicine and your headaches start or they become much worse, it could be the medication that's the problem. Ask your doctor about this. He may be able to give you a different medication or reduce the dosage of the drug. If it is a blood pressure medication that you take, having a list of blood pressure readings, particularly if they correlate to your headaches, will be very helpful information for your doctor.

Question 11: Daily Use of Over-the-Counter (OTC) or Prescribed Headache Drugs

If you're taking Excedrin, Tylenol, or aspirin every day, this could be the cause of your headaches. Rebound headaches, which we discussed in Chapter 2, are headaches that are caused by taking headache medicines. It takes about two weeks to resolve this problem and you need your doctor to help you. Don't just stop the medication on your own, because you'll probably develop an extremely bad headache, even worse than what you're used to. Some prescribed drugs can lead to rebound headaches, such as Cafergot (ergotamine). Find out more about rebound headaches in Chapter 9.

Question 12: Smoking Causes (or Worsens) Headaches

If you smoke, you should stop smoking now, to significantly improve your chronic headache problem and also limit your risk for developing many severe health problems. (Lung cancer and oral cancer are only two of the many serious illnesses caused by smoking.) Some researchers report that smoking is a particular trigger for those who suffer from chronic cluster headaches, although people with any type of headache may be prone to develop a headache from tobacco smoke.

If you stop smoking, once you've gotten past the withdrawal stage—which can often be eased by nicotine replacement products or medications such as Zyban (bupropion)—you are likely to find your headaches will be less frequent and less intense. It's probably the nicotine (the addictive substance in tobacco products) that causes or worsens headaches, although there are hundreds of other harmful substances in cigarettes and other tobacco products. You're better off without them all.

Question 13: Exercise as a Headache Trigger

If you exercise frequently it's possible that exercising may be one of your headache triggers. Research in gender differences between men and women who suffer from chronic headaches (reported in *Headache* in 2001), indicated that men were more likely to report exercise as a trigger than women.

This doesn't mean you should stop exercising, but may mean that you should take preventive action. For example, if you're prone to migraines after an active game of handball, you may wish to take a preventive medication before you start the game, or you may wish to substitute a different exercise to see if your body will better tolerate a change in your routine by giving you fewer (or no) headaches. For example, instead of playing handball, consider swimming or taking a long walk. (Walking is an excellent and much underrated exercise.)

Question 14: That Certain Smell— Odor Headache Triggers

Some people who suffer from headaches, especially migraines, may develop a headache after exposure to certain odors, such as heavy perfume, tobacco smoke, or gasoline. The next time you're around one of these odors, make a note and then see whether a headache ensues within a few hours.

What if it does? If your significant other loves perfume, but you think it may give you a severe headache, ask him or her to go easy or go without, and then see if your headaches decrease in number and wane in intensity. If they do, tell your partner that the perfume is causing you headaches and you'd really appreciate it if he or she would use less or none around you. And keep in mind that you should not wear perfume either! You have limited control over other people, but you can certainly refrain from using a headache-inducing product yourself. You may also wish to buy odor-free deodorant and laundry detergents.

The smell of tobacco smoke may cause headaches, and this is yet another reason to stop smoking, as it is for your family members who smoke. As for gasoline odors, most gas stations are self-service, but you can turn your head away from the gas-pump nozzle you insert in your car when you fuel up. Or ask a family member to pump the gas for you.

Keeping a Headache-Trigger Diary

If you're not sure what triggers your headaches, consider keeping a trigger diary to help you, as seen in our sample on page 56. You can photocopy our chart or draw up your own, using a simple school notebook. Or ask your physician if he has a headache diary format that he favors. Such a diary can provide you and your doctor with a record of when your headaches occurred. Keep in mind that there's a time lag between when you encounter a trigger, whether it's bright light, loud noise, food, or something else, and when the headache actually occurs. For some people, the headache may occur almost immediately, but for others, the lag could be several hours or longer.

For simplicity, we have included several major headache triggers for you to track. However, if you know or suspect that you

FIGURE 3.1 Sample Headache-Trigger Diary

Day	Headache Y/N	Weather*	Foods**	Bright Light/Loud Noise	Stress Levels (1–5)	Medication Changes
Sun						
Mon						
Tues						
Wed						
Thurs						
Fri						
Sat						

*Very sunny, moderate, rainy, or cold or hot temperatures

**Salty or fruity foods

may have a problem with a trigger that's not listed in the chart, then add that trigger to your own chart.

Using Your Trigger Diary

Make a notation in your headache chart *every* day, even if you don't have a headache. Sometimes the information you gain on nonheadache days can be as valuable as what you discover about the days when you *do* get headaches. For example, if you don't have a headache on Sunday, and you've noted that the weather was moderate (not really sunny, but not raining either); but then on Wednesday it's raining like crazy, it's very hot, and you have a five-alarm headache, you may be weather-sensitive.

What temperatures are hot or cold? It depends on your personal response. If you're cold when it's 60 degrees out, it doesn't matter if your sister isn't cold at that temperature. *You* are cold, so mark it down on your chart as a cold day.

In the foods column, note whether you ate any foods that were spicy, salty, or fruity. Also, write down if you ate anything new or unfamiliar to you. For example, maybe sushi is all wrong for you, especially when you get a terrible headache a few hours later.

Keep in mind that there may be up to a 12-hour lag between when you eat something and when you develop a headache. Also, annotate in the food section whether you consumed *any* alcohol (even one glass of wine counts), as alcohol is a major headache trigger for many people.

In the next column, on bright lights and extreme noise, write down if you were exposed to one or both of these problems, each day. If not, simply write "no" for that day. But if, for example, your office was being remodeled and people were drilling and pounding all day, then that constitutes a "yes/sound." (Be sure to put down both the "yes" and the "sound," because it's easy to forget and when you go back to look at the diary, you may think you were exposed to intense light that day instead of extreme sound.)

In the column on stress levels, each day, record your overall stress level, on a scale of 1 to 5, with 1 being not bad and 5 being extremely bad stress. Again, you decide how stressed-out you are, and rate yourself accordingly for the day.

In the last column on medication changes, write down if you are taking any new medications or if the dosages of your regular medications have been changed, either up or down.

Keep your trigger diary for at least two weeks and then take a look at it, looking for patterns of when you had headaches and when you didn't have them. As you gain experience, you'll get better at identifying your triggers. And once those culprits are identified, you can work on either avoiding them or adapting to them.

PART II

The Cervicogenic Headache: A Real Pain in the Neck

In this section, we provide important information on the cervicogenic headache, a common but frequently undiagnosed headache caused by a problem in the neck, upper spine, or shoulder. We cover the basics on "neck" headaches (such as who suffers from them and why—ranging from arthritis, to joint disease, to whiplash, and more) as well as useful medications and therapies that help with chronic pain (such as trigger injections, massage therapy, chiropractic care and, if necessary, surgery). We also include simple effective exercises for neck headache sufferers, to increase neck strength and flexibility. Finally, you'll find out how to prevent cervicogenic headaches by the actions you take at home or work, such as changing your use of the phone and computer. Wouldn't you rather *not* have these headaches? Then read this section!

CHAPTER 4

The Basics on Neck Headaches

Diana was diagnosed with migraines ten years ago, and she'd also been wondering for most of those years if there was anything more that could be done to help her. The migraine medication that the doctor had prescribed took some of the edge off of her pain, but it really didn't give her that much relief. And the terrible headaches always returned later, no matter what she did. She kept her stress levels down, stayed away from foods like red wine and aged cheese, and pretty much filled every directive for migraine avoidance that she could find. But the severe pain kept coming back. Not only would the pain come back, but recently the number of headaches Diana was suffering from had increased from one or two each week to three or four per week. It was becoming nearly impossible for her to lead a normal life.

Then one day when the pain was very bad and she'd somehow run out of her migraine medication, Diana called her doctor's office. She was told that her regular physician was ill and would be out of the office for at least a few weeks, so Diana found us, called our office, and she was given an emergency appointment to see me (Dr. Sudderth). Despite her severe pain and the major struggle to concentrate as she talked to me through her headache, Diana gave me a complete medical history. She told me about her migraines and how she'd been having such a difficult time for so long. I prescribed some of her regular medication, but also insisted on doing a complete new workup on her, and told Diana that she'd also need to come in for some laboratory tests and imaging tests soon, on one of her nonheadache days.

I examined Diana's neck and noted that the muscles were extremely contracted and very tight. In fact, when I gently examined Diana in the neck and shoulders, she winced from the pain; and I noticed that she had severely restricted movement in her neck as well. I ordered laboratory tests for thyroid disease, diabetes, and other possible problems that Diana might have, and also ordered a magnetic resonance imaging (MRI) scan of her head and neck. When the results came in, I saw that the laboratory findings were all normal, but the MRI showed there was some severe arthritis in Diana's neck.

At Diana's follow-up appointment, I told her that I was reasonably confident that she was suffering from cervicogenic headaches, a headache type caused by referred pain, in this case generated from a problem in the neck. I also told Diana that treatment of the true source of her underlying problem was the only way to resolve her headache pain. I had a preliminary plan to test my theory, if she was willing to try it. Diana told me that she was starting to develop a headache, right there in the office, and she assured me that she was ready to try anything that might help cut back on those horrible headaches. With her permission, I tested my theory that Diana's chronic headache problem was probably generated by pain in her neck, by injecting lidocaine into several areas around the bunched up muscles that were easily visible. (These were also the same areas in her neck where Diana had cringed when I had examined her.) Within moments, I could see visible results: the muscles were relaxing. And Diana's headache? It was gone.

I told Diana that the headache problem might not recur, but it could very well come back again in a few days or a week. However, now we both knew what worked, so it was treatable. I also said that I could also inject other medications into the cervical spine, such as corticosteroids, which would provide longer-term relief, and there were other remedies as well that could alleviate the pain from her overly tense neck muscles. In addition, I told Diana she should periodically check her neck area to feel for herself if the muscles seemed to be starting to bunch up, and if so, she needed to take the preventive actions that I'd recommend.

Not everyone responds to the lidocaine injections as readily as Diana did; she was fortunate. A nonresponse to trigger injections doesn't mean that you *don't* have cervicogenic headaches. But it's also true that many people with cervicogenic headaches go undiagnosed for years, or sometimes indefinitely. This is one of the major points we're trying to convey here, and we think it's time that situation changed.

The topic of cervicogenic headaches is so important to us that we are devoting three chapters of this book to it. We have treated hundreds of patients like Diana with cervicogenic headaches, and the majority responded very well to treatment. If you have chronic headaches that have not responded to treatment (despite the name that has been attached to your headaches, such as migraines or tension-type headaches), it's possible that you too may be suffering from cervicogenic headaches.

And don't think that you would somehow *know* if you were. Why would you? If many physicians aren't yet aware of cervicogenic headaches (and they aren't), why would patients be expected to know about them? In addition, for most of our patients, their head pain was so severe that they didn't even notice their neck pain until we gently examined the area.

What Is a Cervicogenic Headache?

A cervicogenic (or neck) headache is an extremely common headache that is usually caused by arthritis, degenerative disk disease, or muscle spasms in the neck—although there are other causes of the headache, such as whiplash, that we discuss in this chapter. Ottar Sjaastad and his colleagues first published a medical journal article on the cervicogenic headache in 1983, and he later refined the diagnostic criteria in 1998. The International Headache Society has also developed criteria for the cervicogenic headache.

In general, the cervicogenic headache is a headache that stems from pain in the neck or shoulder that is primarily or solely experienced in the forehead, temples, and/or the eye area (orbital region). This pain is often exacerbated by static neck positions (keeping your neck in the exact same position for a long time) or by special neck movements (such as trying to use your head and neck to hold the telephone rather then using a headset, or simply holding the telephone with your hand). With the cervicogenic headache, there is also either tenderness in the neck area, changes in the contour of the neck muscle, or a painful response to the stretching and contracting of the neck muscles. Dr. Sjaastad believed that if the headache responds to nerve blocks given in the cervical area, it is then, by definition, a cervicogenic headache— although some experts dispute this criterion.

If imaging studies of the neck and spine show abnormalities, they may reveal an abnormal posture or bone abnormalities, such as *scoliosis* (curvature of the spine). One of the most common findings on X-ray or MRI is the loss of the normal curvature or a straightening of the neck spine. (There is usually a gentle curve in healthy individuals but in those with cervicogenic headaches, there is a vertical alignment of the spine—straight up and down.) Imaging studies may also reveal abnormal movements when your head or neck is extended or flexed (when your head is up or down as far as you can make it go). Fractures, osteoarthritis, or other bone and tissue abnormalities may also be present.

Many doctors see the cervicogenic headache as more of a syndrome than a disease, in that there are many diseases and disorders that are associated with the cervicogenic headache, such as arthritis, degenerative disk disease, and whiplash or other traumatic injuries. However, the headache itself may be the primary or sometimes the *only* indication that a problem exists.

As discussed in Chapter 3, patients with cervicogenic headaches may find that their headaches are triggered by intense light or loud noise. Since patients with migraines also have these very same triggers, this is yet another reason why the cervicogenic headache isn't always diagnosed, and instead, many patients with these headaches are misdiagnosed with migraines or tension-type headaches. Complicating the issue further, most people with cervicogenic headaches periodically *do* have migraines or tension-type headaches, in addition to their cervicogenic headaches. As a

Who Gets Neck Headaches?

Estimates of how many people develop chronic cervicogenic headaches vary considerably. In one study of headache patients, about 18 percent had cervicogenic headaches. In another study, reported in the *Clinical Journal of Pain* in 2001, the researchers analyzed patients who visited their pain clinic. Of 1,466 chronic pain patients with different types of pain problems, 153 had severe headaches. The researchers found that about a third of the patients had cervicogenic headaches; however, many had other headache types as well. The cervicogenic patients were an average age of 45 years, and 39 percent said their headache was so severe that it woke them up in the morning. Among this group, the two headache precipitants reported most often were neck position (67.3 percent) and mental stress (65.4 percent).

result, the diagnosis can be a challenging one for doctors, so you need an experienced physician who has an interest in treating headache patients.

Some types of headaches are more gender-specific; for example, women are much more prone to developing migraines than men, while men are more likely to suffer from cluster headaches than women. Cervicogenic headaches occur in women more frequently, by at least a 2-to-1 ratio and some experts believe it is 3-to-1. Why do more women develop cervicogenic headaches than men? No one knows.

Children may also develop cervicogenic headaches, sometimes because of the heavy and poorly designed backpacks they lug back and forth from school. If you have children, you should weigh your child's backpack. If it's 10 pounds or more (depending on his age and size), work with his teachers on finding a more healthy solution, such as keeping an extra set of schoolbooks at home or switching to a rolling backpack that is like carry-on luggage.

Interestingly, many doctors mistakenly believe that all cervicogenic headaches are really just tension headaches. That is not what the researchers in the *Clinical Journal of Pain* found in their study. Instead, they found little overlap between patients with both tension headaches and cervicogenic headaches (17.3 percent). In contrast, many cervicogenic headache patients had both cervicogenic headaches and migraine with aura (71.2 percent) or migraine without aura (73.1 percent). (Many patients suffered from *both* migraines with and without aura.) Apparently there is not much overlap between cervicogenic headaches and cluster headaches: the percentage of patients with both cervicogenic headaches and cluster headaches was 7.7 percent.

How Can Pain in Your Neck Make Your Head Hurt?

As discussed, the cervicogenic headache is a form of referred pain, which means the cause of the pain is distant from where you actually experience it in your head. Many people have had dental pain that they were convinced was caused by a specific tooth, but the actual pain generator was another tooth. Or maybe the teeth were all fine but the sinuses draining into the teeth were causing dental pain. Some people have had a tooth extracted, not knowing that their underlying problem was really sinusitis or another nondental issue.

Referred pain is a very common phenomenon, although it seems odd to people. Yet, many people understand the referred pain of a heart attack, radiating pain into the left arm or the jaw when there is nothing wrong with the arm or jaw. The pain sensors for the heart are some of the same ones that send messages to these areas.

What mechanism can cause pain to be experienced in a site that's distant from the cause of the pain? In the case of the cervicogenic headache, the neurological explanation can be rather dense and complicated. But basically, a problem that occurs in the cervical spine, particularly in the top three vertebrae and especially the second and third vertebrae (C2 and C3), generates pain that is primarily or solely experienced in the head.

For example, the pain may travel from the trapezius muscle in the shoulder and lower head and be magnified by several times or more in the occipitofrontal muscle in your head, where the headache pain is experienced. Sometimes the pain signals travel to the temporal muscle of the head, and that's where your headache pain is experienced.

The trigeminal nerve in the cheekbone area of your face may sometimes be the conduit for pain that is referred from your neck. This nerve descends to the trigeminocervical nucleus (basically, a relay station) located at C3 in the spine. It then loops back up to another relay station in the deep central part of the brain to be interpreted as pain.

These are only a few examples of ways that a problem in the neck can ultimately lead to headache pain. Some experts believe that pain in the lower cervical disks (there are seven cervical disks in all) can ultimately lead to cervicogenic headaches. It is also possible that pain emanating from other disks or vertebrae, such as in the thoracic spine (the middle of your back) or the lumbar spine (the lower back) can cause cervicogenic headaches, although experts disagree on this issue.

Causes of Cervicogenic Headaches

We've talked about possible ways that the transmission of pain occurs. But why does it happen at all? What sets the pain process in motion? People develop cervicogenic headaches for many different reasons, including muscle spasms in the cervical (upper spine) area of the back, arthritis, whiplash from a car crash, and an injury caused by a fall.

Keep in mind that the cause may be detached in time from the result. What we mean by this is that you may have been in a car accident six months or a year ago, and your chronic headaches are increasing now rather than decreasing. It's also true that sometimes an untreated injury can become aggravated over the course of time. Or you may have had osteoarthritis for years, and only now has it devolved to the point of causing your severe chronic headaches that were generated by neck pain. Degenerative disk disease is another cause of cervicogenic headaches.

Whiplash

If you've been a car crash victim at any point, you may have suffered from what is commonly called *whiplash*. This condition is the subject of a lot of litigation; and while it is often considered controversial, it is a valid medical problem. Many whiplash patients recover with treatment within days or weeks; while in other cases, the condition may persist for months or years. Whiplash often leads to severe and sometimes chronic headaches. Some of the worst headaches we have seen in our practice were posttraumatic in nature.

What Is Whiplash and Who Suffers from It? According to the National Institute of Neurological Disorders and Stroke, whiplash causes soft tissue neck injury; and it usually results from a car accident—particularly one in which the car was rear-ended—often at a low speed. Some studies indicate that passengers are at greater risk than drivers; and while whiplash is more likely to occur if you don't wear your seat belt, even belted drivers or passengers may develop whiplash in a violent crash. Women also have a greater risk of suffering from whiplash, although no one knows why it works out this way.

There are about 800,000 to a million whiplash injuries each year in the United States. Most patients recover, although up to 80 percent suffer from some temporary headache and neck pain. Some studies have shown that about 60 percent continue to suffer from headaches for a year or longer, although experts disagree on the overall percentage of patients who experience long-term damage. Of course, even if the percentage were very small, if you're a person diagnosed with whiplash, the problem looms very large in your life.

The recovery from whiplash is longer in individuals who have had a prior history of neck pain and/or headaches before the accident occurred, as well as those who suffer from muscle pain or pain or numbness that extends from the neck to the shoulders, arms, and hands. Patients who had their heads turned or inclined at the point of impact in the car crash often have more severe whiplash symptoms. This means, for example, if the passenger was looking out the side window, she'd be at greater risk for suffering from whiplash and cervicogenic headaches than if she were looking straight ahead when the accident occurred. Of course, whether one is looking straight ahead or has one's head turned at the time of a crash is just luck.

Whiplash may also occur from a diving accident or other accident causing excessive extension and hyperflexion of the neck. Adults who suffer from whiplash are more likely to suffer from neck trauma, headaches, and other symptoms.

Whiplash Symptoms. The pain that ensues from a whiplash injury stems from the fact that at the point of impact from the crash, your head was violently thrown forward and then backward (or backward and then forward), causing severe stress on the bones, disks, and muscles in your upper spine. The patient may feel pain in the head, neck, shoulders, and arms and may suffer damage to the muscles, ligaments, and/or vertebrae.

Headache is a common symptom of whiplash, along with neck pain. Patients may also experience:

- Shoulder pain and/or back pain
- Dizziness and some confusion, along with the head pain
- Nausea and double vision
- Problems with concentration

In addition to these symptoms, frequently patients will complain of an imbalance or illusion of movement, although some can have true vertigo (a spinning sensation).

Whiplash and Cervicogenic Headaches. Whiplash can definitely cause chronic cervicogenic headaches, because of the damage that occurs to the muscles and tendons in the neck and shoulders. The

Why Diagnosis of Whiplash Can Be Difficult

Although physicians will usually order *magnetic resonance imaging* (*MRI*) or *computerized tomography* (*CT*) scans to detect any evidence of fracture, sprains, or other trauma, the MRI may not detect any evidence of whiplash, even when the patient is clearly suffering and isn't faking. This is because of the microscopic and sometimes undetectable damage that may occur and can cause profound suffering in patients. (Although there are some patients who really are exaggerating their injuries, doctors can usually identify them by their excessive reactions.) Cadaver/autopsy studies have found microscopic hemorrhages on examination of the neck muscles. Obviously, this type of detailed examination cannot be done on living patients.

Some researchers have found brain abnormalities in whiplash patients by using advanced imaging techniques that are not available to most physicians, such as *positron-emission tomography* (*PET*) scans or *single photon emission computed tomography* (*SPECT*) scans. MRI with spectroscopy has been shown to be helpful in illuminating these problems. Since most readers won't have access to these tools, the usefulness of the information lies solely in that whiplash has been documented to be a valid problem. What this boils down to, very simply, is that if you're suffering from whiplash, even though your tests are normal, your pain is real. You're entitled to real pain relief, and if you're not getting it from your current physician, then you need to find another doctor.

pain may start immediately or it may be delayed by 24 or more hours from the time of the car crash. Often it takes up to 4–5 days for the symptoms to present themselves. This is partly because of *delayed onset myofascial syndrome* (*DOMS*). That is, it may take a few days for the tissue swelling and damage to continue, leading to a slow increase in headache pain. Headaches are common, and when whiplash pain lasts more than six months, it's considered a chronic medical problem.

Treating Headaches Generated by Whiplash. In a severe case of whiplash, patients may be advised to wear a soft cervical collar for several weeks, to immobilize the neck. However, recent studies have indicated that physical therapy and neck exercises are much more effective than the former old ways of bed rest and cervical collars. Physical therapy may help, as may massage therapy, heat, and medications. (Chapter 5 includes information on physical therapy and other treatment methods.) Progressing to an exercise strengthening program, particularly one that targets the cervical muscles that were injured, can help the patient regain the strength and range of motion that were lost.

Other Injuries

Have you had any falls, even ones that you considered minor? Although often you can tell right away if you're injured after a fall, especially if you've fractured any bones, it's also true that a fall can create damage that you *don't* notice immediately. Subtle damage can continue to erode your muscles and tissues and later may result in the development of cervicogenic headaches. You need not have fallen directly on your head or neck for a problem to occur. For example, if you landed on your buttocks very hard in a sitting position, such as in a fall on a slippery floor or on an icy sidewalk, the jarring impact can rapidly slam down your entire spine. This can apply enormous force that leads to damage to your neck, and consequently, to cervicogenic headaches.

If you've been involved in any physical altercations with others or you were the victim of abuse, including physical abuse that occurred as a child, then you may also be prone to suffering from cervicogenic headaches.

Some Exercises and Sports Can Cause Headaches

Some exercises and sports (such as scuba diving or rock climbing) that cause hyperflexion or hyperextension of the neck can lead to cervicogenic headaches. This is not a common cause of these headaches; however, if you already know that you suffer from cervicogenic headaches, it's best to talk to your doctor before you attempt scuba diving or rock climbing, as you don't want to worsen your condition. You should probably also think twice about performing demanding gymnastics and any other sports that would require extreme movements of your head and neck. Limiting your activities at an amusement park may also be a good idea; yes, those signs on rides that say, "If you are pregnant or have a spine condition, you may not want to ride. . ." are directed at patients with cervicogenic headache problems as well as other spine problems.

Arthritic Problems

Nearly everyone over age 40 has some osteoarthritis in their cervical spine from basic wear and tear that occurs in life, but some individuals have a more advanced case than others. It's partly a genetic problem; so if your parents and/or siblings have arthritis, then usually you're at risk, too. (Don't be too hard on them. You inherited some of their good qualities too!)

Arthritis in the spine increases the risk for cervicogenic headaches. *Nonsteroidal anti-inflammatory drugs (NSAIDs)* may help, as may heat and massage therapy, and there are also good preventive actions that you can take. (In Chapter 6, we offer recommendations on effective ways to prevent cervicogenic headaches, whatever the cause.)

Degenerative Disk Disease

The disks in your back are like shock-absorbing pads that lie between each vertebra in the spine. Sometimes these disks are harmed by a car crash or other injury, but disks can also get worn away from aging. Most people age 40 and older have some disk degeneration that's apparent on an X-ray or imaging scan. We liken damaged disks to a jelly doughnut that has been slightly pressed down, so that a little (or a lot) of the jelly is leaking out the sides of the doughnut. When the disks degenerate and the "jelly" leaks out it means the disk is herniated.

It's also true that the disks may not be herniated, but they are bulging out (sort of resembling the fat of "love handles" on an overweight person's waist). This condition may be a sort of "prequel" to the future greater deterioration of the disks and the ultimate complication of a herniated disk. However, even without herniation, bulging disks may cause severe pain, although the condition isn't painful to everyone. (Sometimes bulging disks are diagnosed on routine X-rays, but if the patient has no complaints, there's no reason for any treatment.)

Degenerative disk disease can lead to cervicogenic headaches. Treatments include medications, exercises, massage therapy, and, if the condition is severe, surgery to remove the disk or other surgical procedures, which we cover more in Chapter 5.

Many people with degenerative disk disease also suffer from arthritis, particularly osteoarthritis. This compound problem, particularly when it occurs in the cervical spine, increases the risk for a patient developing chronic cervicogenic headaches.

When Causes Are Unknown

Doctors can't always pinpoint *why* you have a medical problem, even after exhaustive tests. Sometimes the best that physicians can do is to determine *what* your problem is when the why of it eludes them, despite their best efforts. This is true for the cervicogenic headache as well as for many other medical problems. As a result, we may know or strongly suspect that your pain stems from the neck, but we still may not know why you're having this pain.

However, knowing that your headache pain's probable origin is your neck is useful information and we doctors can work from that basis. For example, the neck exercises, therapies, and medications that usually work well for patients with whiplash or joint or disk disease are often effective treatments for cervicogenic headaches of unknown causes. Electrical stimulators (discussed further in Chapter 13) that therapists use, now available for home use with a physician's prescription, are another extremely effective way to treat this problem.

Symptoms and Signs of Neck Headaches

Could you be suffering from cervicogenic headaches? Your doctor must be the one to make this call, but there are some indications that you can consider and ask your doctor about. The key symptoms of neck headaches are the following:

- Tenderness upon the physician's examination of the neck
- Minor neck pain that becomes severe head pain
- Pain that increases with sitting or lying down for several hours
- Limited flexibility of the neck
- Headache pain that occurs upon extra neck movements or pressure on the neck
- Shoulder pain

Tenderness or Pain in the Neck or Shoulders upon Examination

Most of the patients we diagnose with cervicogenic pain didn't complain to us about neck pain and were solely concerned with their chronic severe headaches. In fact, it's fair to say that the majority of these patients didn't even notice that their neck hurt so much until we examined them, gently pressing on the upper spine and shoulder area, and eliciting facial winces of pain and some verbal ouches.

The reason for this unawareness of their neck pain is that the headache pain was so overwhelmingly bad it made the neck pain either unnoticeable to patients or just a minor aggravation to them. Understandably, they were shocked to learn that neck pain was the source of their head pain.

I (Dr. Kandel), recently had a patient, Emily, who had been seen by her family doctor for over two years. She was on large amounts of nar-

cotics, was diagnosed with "migraine headaches," yet still was having nearly daily headaches. She worked in a physician's office, so she had some medical knowledge. When I first saw her, I explained that by definition, she could not have "just" migraines. I agreed to continue her pain management regimen while I searched for her problem. The MRI of her brain was normal, but the MRI of the cervical spine showed a ruptured disk at the level of C4–5 (the fourth and fifth vertebrae in the neck area of the spine), with some instability of the spine. She was sent to the neurosurgeon for surgery and a few weeks later, she had a small surgical incision in the front of her neck, but no more headaches! She has told me repeatedly that having her surgery was "the best trade of my life." She traded in years of pain with one surgical procedure.

Minor Neck Pain That Develops into a Headache

Although many patients with cervicogenic headaches may not notice neck pain, some patients are very aware of it. They report that their neck starts hurting them sometime before they develop a severe headache, saying that it's almost as if the neck pain somehow traveled to the forehead, where the pain then amplified about ten times more. They are right—it did travel to their head from the neck.

Pain That Increases with Maintaining a Position for Several Hours

A common problem among numerous people with chronic cervicogenic headaches is that they are in a holding pattern, position-wise. What we mean is simply that many patients with these frequent headaches sit for many hours, while others are standing or even lying down in the same position for hours. For example, auto mechanics may spend many hours on their backs underneath a car while repairing it. These stationary positions place a lot of strain on the spine, which ultimately translates into neck problems and then headaches. Other common careers that cause this problem include those as plumbers, electricians, nail technicians, computer workers, telephone operators, and store clerks. This is a very limited list of occupations that can lead to neck–related headaches.

Limited Flexibility of the Neck

Researchers who have compared patients with cervicogenic headaches to those with migraines, tension-type headaches, and cluster headaches have found that patients with cervicogenic headaches have significantly less mobility in their neck. It's not just that it hurts them to move their necks, but rather that they *can't* move them as many degrees as people with other forms of headaches or as people with no headaches at all.

In a study reported in 2001 in *Cephalgia*, researchers studied 44 patients with cervicogenic headaches. Twenty of the patients had developed cervicogenic headaches after motor vehicle accidents, and 24 had not been in a car accident. These two groups were compared to each other along with a control group of patients with migraines and a group of subjects without headaches. The cervicogenic headache patients had the least mobility, particularly the patients who had been in car crashes. For example, in considering the flexion/extension of the neck, the average performed by the control subjects was 123 degrees. The migraine patients had a similar range of 125 degrees. In contrast, the cervicogenic headache patients who had not been in a car accident had an average flexion/extension of 114 degrees, while those who had been in an accident averaged the lowest of all (101 degrees).

Special machines such as those produced by MedX have documented the more limited range of motion in cervicogenic headache patients. If your doctor has such equipment (it's expensive and few doctors do have it), then a test of your neck mobility may be sufficient to help diagnose you with cervicogenic headaches. This equipment can also measure strength and compare you to age-matched controls of the same sex, so you can see where your neck stands compared to others.

Headache Pain Stemming from Neck Movements or Pressure on the Neck

Exercises that involve using the neck will often cause or exacerbate the cervicogenic headache. (Although the neck exercises that we propose in Chapter 5 should help build up your flexibility.) For example, some sports that may require craning or hyperextending the neck could lead to a cervicogenic headache. Even watching a tennis game, with the back and forth of the ball, could cause enough neck movement to trigger this type of headache.

Shoulder Pain

Patients with chronic neck headaches may suffer from shoulder pain or sometimes from pain that radiates from the shoulder and into the arm. Not all patients have this symptom and the lack of shoulder pain doesn't mean that these headaches can be ruled out.

Are You at Risk? Diagnosing the Cervicogenic Headache

Many people with degenerative disks in the cervical spine (disks that are bulging out) don't complain of pain; and in those cases, nothing needs to be done other than maintaining good body mechanics and posture. However, if you do have pain in your neck as well as headaches, the doctor needs to rule out a cervical disk problem. This can be accomplished with X-rays, a computerized tomography (CT) scan, or a magnetic resonance imaging (MRI) scan. These are all referred to as imaging tests because they show the radiologist and your doctor what's going on with your bones and the surrounding soft tissues by providing an image of them. It's also true, as mentioned earlier, that your imaging studies could come out normal, even though you really do have a medical problem.

Of course the physical examination is very important too. The doctor needs to observe you and examine you. Here are some areas that may lead the doctor to believe you may be suffering from cervicogenic headaches:

* Your posture
* Your line of work

- Results from your imaging tests
- Tenderness in the neck and shoulder area
- Your minimal (or no) response to treatment for migraine or other forms of headache

Your Posture: Standing and Sitting

For many people, their standard sitting or standing posture is a slumped over position, with the head extended forward rather than erect and over their shoulders. If you're not sure what your posture looks like, try sitting or standing in front of a mirror. (Or have someone take your picture when you least expect it.) And please, don't cheat yourself by sucking it up and standing very tall so you'll look better in the mirror than you normally do! Instead, be realistic, and stand (or sit) in the way that feels natural to you. If it's a slumped position, you'll know you need to work on improving it because this position, especially after several hours and day after day, places a considerable strain on the neck and often leads to neck headaches.

We're not suggesting that you stand at attention like a soldier, but instead, put your shoulders back and hold your head up and see if this eases the pain, even if only a little bit. Be sure to read Chapter 6 for hints on preventing headaches by adjusting your computer, your chair, and other devices.

What You Do for a Living

Some career fields are more likely to lead to neck pain and cervicogenic headaches than others. Studies have shown that truck drivers are more prone to neck pain, so it's not surprising to us when we diagnose neck headaches in people who are truck drivers.

But you can also be a white-collar worker, such as an attorney, a computer programmer, an editor, or even a doctor, and face an increased risk for developing cervicogenic headaches. It's not your education level that is the key issue but rather your physical position when you perform whatever it is that your job requires. If it's a job that is mostly comprised of tasks that are achieved when you're sitting down (as with truck driving or writing computer programs), then your risk is increased for neck headaches.

In addition, if you perform a job that requires repetitive tasks, you may also be at risk for cervicogenic headaches, especially if it requires constant repetitive movement of your head and neck. A person working on an assembly line who must move their neck all the time may be at risk, as are musicians who must move their neck about constantly. If you feel like a bobble-head doll at work because you're always moving your neck up, down, and around to accomplish your job, then you're at risk for developing cervicogenic headaches.

Mothers of babies and young children may develop cervicogenic headaches. Constantly picking up your baby and carrying her around, even when she weighs 20 pounds, can lead to neck pain and then to these headaches. (Read our suggestions for mothers of babies and small children in Chapter 6.)

Results from Your Imaging Tests

The doctor will check your X-rays and computerized tomography (CT) scan or magnetic resonance imaging (MRI) scan to see if there are any indications of arthritis, disk disease, or any problems in the cervical spine. These imaging studies can be very revealing and helpful in showing the doctor where the primary problem areas are. They may also be completely normal.

Little or No Response to Other Headache Treatments

Some people have been treated for years for other headache types, particularly migraines, tension-type headaches, and sinus headaches. But, as with Diana at the beginning of this chapter, they obtained little or no relief from these medications. And why was that? For the underlying reason that their pain-generating problem wasn't brain pain; instead, it was pain stemming from a problem in the cervical spine.

If your headaches have been going on for years and your treatments so far aren't helping you, we recommend that you ask your doctor to consider whether you may have cervicogenic headaches. Or get a second opinion from another physician, particularly a neurologist, as neurologists are the most likely to be knowledgeable about these headaches. Then be sure to go back and read Chapter 2 on how to find a good physician and the questions you should ask her.

CHAPTER 5

Resolving the Neck Headache

Here's the chapter that many readers may turn to first. It's where we tell you what to *do* about your painful cervicogenic headaches. You can't solve the problem on your own, of course; you'll need to work closely with your doctor. For example, most readers will need to take prescribed medication, at least occasionally. You may also benefit from steroid injections, Botox injections, and other treatments—such as chiropractic, physical therapy, or massage therapy. Some patients may need minor or more serious surgery to combat their pain. You'll also need your doctor to monitor how you're doing, headache-wise and health-wise. And if you are anything like our patients, you will need your doctor to tell you if the latest remedy described in the local paper or talked about at the church social is appropriate for you.

There are many actions that you and your doctor can do to improve your overall headache situation, when it comes to headaches that stem from neck pain. (We also offer preventive solutions in Chapter 6 as well as some good preventive ideas for people with other headache types in Chapter 13. Many of the ideas in both chapters may benefit you considerably, so don't skip either chapter!)

Considering Medications

People with chronic cervicogenic headaches usually need to take medication, and they often need more than one drug to control their symptoms, such as a nonsteroidal anti-inflammatory drug (NSAID).

NSAIDS and Muscle Relaxants

Medications such as NSAIDs and muscle relaxants are common treatments for chronic cervicogenic headaches. We'll mention them briefly here, but we include much more detailed information on each of these individual medications, their side effects, and who should and shouldn't take them (as well as other prescription and over-the-counter medications) in Chapter 11.

Over-the-counter NSAIDs such as ibuprofen or a prescribed NSAID, such as Orudis (ketoprofen), Anaprox (naproxen sodium), or Feldene (piroxicam) may help to control the overall inflammation and pain of your headache. But unfortunately, if you take NSAIDs on a regular basis, you run the risk of developing a stomach ulcer. Contrary to popular belief, extreme stress is not the main cause of ulcers. Instead, it's constant use of NSAIDs and/or infection with a common organism, *Helicobacter pylori* that causes gastric ulcers. (Of course, once you have an ulcer, heightened stress makes you feel worse.) Chronic use of NSAIDs may increase the risk of cardiovascular disease and, in 2005, the FDA ordered labeling changes on them. Read more about this in Chapter 10.

Muscle relaxants may also be ordered by your doctor to treat your pain from cervicogenic headaches, including such drugs as Soma (carisprodol) or Flexeril (cyclobenzaprine). Lioresal or Kemstro (baclofen) are other commonly prescribed drugs in this class.

In cases of severe and unremitting pain—when Tylenol just isn't cutting it for you—you may need a strong analgesic (painkiller), up to and including narcotic medications such as Percocet or hydrocodone. Of course, doctors generally hesitate to prescribe narcotics because some patients can develop a problem with addiction. This happens far more rarely among patients with severe pain than you'd think from articles in the popular press, but it does happen occasionally. However, even without the risk of addiction, narcotics have major side effects, such as extreme constipation and lethargy.

Antidepressants

Some patients with cervicogenic headaches gain improvement from their chronic pain with low dosages of tricyclic antidepressants, such as Elavil (amitriptyline), Pamelor, or Aventyl (which are each forms of nortriptyline). These drugs are sedating and can also help you sleep.

If your doctor prescribes Elavil or a related antidepressant for you, it doesn't automatically mean that he thinks you're depressed. To treat depression, you would usually need to take a much higher dose of the drug than the dosage that is prescribed for chronic pain problems. (It's also possible to have both depression and cervicogenic headaches, in which case a therapeutic dose of an antidepressant would be indicated.)

Preventive Medications

Many patients with cervicogenic headaches take preventive medications, such as Tegretol (carbamazepine) or Topamax (topiramate), which are anti-seizure drugs. Topamax has been proven in research studies to be effective at preventing the chronic pain of headaches in many people, particularly migraines and cluster headaches, but many doctors find it's also effective in preventing cervicogenic headaches. As with all medications, Topamax may have some side effects, including tingling in the fingers and toes, a sense of fogginess or spaciness, or fatigue. However, one noted side effect may be weight loss, and we take advantage of this in our overweight patients who suffer from headaches.

Over-the-Counter and Prescribed Topical Remedies

Many patients with cervicogenic headaches use over-the-counter (OTC) creams to block the muscle pain emanating from the neck, and there are numerous brands available on the market. Most contain lidocaine and some contain capsaicin or other numbing substances. These drugs work to numb the muscular pain occurring just below the surface of the skin.

Some patients benefit greatly from Lidoderm, which is a prescribed lidocaine skin patch (it has a higher level of medication than available in OTC brands). It disperses lidocaine through the skin and into the nerve endings. You may have heard (or maybe you've even tried) transdermal patches for other purposes, such as nicotine patches to help you quit smoking or estrogen patches used by some women with symptoms of menopause, such as hot flashes. Because medication that's given transdermally is absorbed through the skin, it bypasses the stomach; consequently, patients avoid the gastric pain that can be caused by many drugs, such as NSAIDs.

The patches are large (about 5 inches by 7 inches) and can be cut into smaller strips before removing the protective covering and placing them on your skin where you're experiencing pain. To use Lidoderm, you simply place the patch or patches in the areas where you're experiencing pain, whether it's mostly your neck, shoulders, or upper back. You can also use the entire strip, if your pain is spread out over your spine.

Botox for Neck Headaches

Botox is another therapy for patients with chronic cervicogenic headaches, and you may benefit from Botox injections. Research has shown that some patients with cervicogenic headaches show significant improvement after receiving Botox injections. For example, in one study (reported in *Headache* in 2000) of 26 patients with cervicogenic headaches caused by whiplash, 14 received Botox injections and 12 received saline injections. At the two- and four-week point, the patients who had received Botox had significant improvements in their pain levels as well as in their range of motion when compared to the placebo group that received the saline.

However, some studies have shown only mixed results with Botox among patients with cervicogenic headaches, and some doctors limit Botox use to their migraine patients, where there is much more supporting research on its effectiveness. If spasm is a major component of your problem, or severely restricted range of motion is present, then Botox may be ideal for you. Sometimes patients with chronic cervicogenic headaches who have not responded to any other treatments that their doctor has tried will show a dramatic response to just one Botox injection. The effect will usually wear off eventually, and the patient will generally need another injection in three or four months.

Our own patients with cervicogenic headaches and other forms of headaches, such as migraines, have shown a marked improvement after receiving Botox injections. In fact, we have devoted an entire chapter, Chapter 12, to this subject because we consider it such an important and timely topic.

Trigger Injections

We mentioned a bit earlier that certain OTCs contain lidocaine and can be helpful in treating cervicogenic headaches. In addition, many patients benefit from receiving trigger point injections of lidocaine and related anesthetic drugs or corticosteroids into the area around the muscles surrounding the upper cervical spine. Trigger injections are usually given in a series of shots injected into and around the muscles where you're experiencing the most pain. Relief usually comes quickly (within hours) or not at all. But doctors can't know ahead of time if trigger injections will work for you; the only way to find out is to try them.

Most physicians spray the area that is to be injected with numbing medication. You may feel a little pain later on at the injection site, when the numbing medication wears off, but it will hopefully be countered by the major relief you gain from the lessening of your headache pain. When the area is sufficiently numb, the injection will be made and you'll feel a mild pinprick or sometimes a slightly stronger sensation.

Lidocaine and related drugs are often used in trigger injections of the muscles. However, some patients improve with depot (long-lasting) intramuscular injections of steroids, such as methylprednisolone. This drug may provide pain relief for from ten days to three months, depending on the patient.

Joint Injections

Doctors have used joint injections of steroids to relieve neck and back pain for years, and they are often very effective—although the pain generally comes back in 3–4 months for most patients. Rather than injecting the drug into muscles, as with trigger injections, the physician injects the medication directly into the affected joint or its nerve supply.

Doctors usually inject a corticosteroid drug, which has an anti-inflammatory effect and makes the overly tensed muscles relax. The injections can usually be performed in the doctor's office and the procedure takes about 20 minutes from start to finish. Plan ahead and bring someone with you to drive you home, just in case you need some extra help.

The Nerve Block

A nerve block is another alternative for the patient with frequent cervicogenic headaches. In this procedure, anesthetic and/or steroid medications are injected to block the pain at the site of the offending nerve, usually at the location of the second or third cervical disk. The doctor uses a fluoroscope and sometimes an MRI to provide him with guidance on where to inject the patient. Doctors can also do this procedure using a computerized tomography (CT) scanner. The nerve blocks seem to be most successful if there is some degree of radiating or referred pain. We advise our patients to have someone drive them home, as this procedure can lead to some discomfort for a day or two.

Rubbing Out the Pain: Massage Therapy

If you're in the throes of a severe headache, massage therapy usually is a bad idea. But if the headache has just started or you'd like

Studies Support Joint Injections

Many studies have demonstrated that injections of steroids into the joints can bring major pain relief to patients. In one small study of 18 patients with chronic headaches that stemmed from whiplash to the cervical spine, reported in a 2001 issue of the *American Journal of Physical Medicine & Rehabilitation*, the patients were treated with facet (zygapophyseal) joint injections of a mixture of corticosteroids. Facet joints are located in various parts of the cervical spine as well as in other parts of the backbone. The patients had previously suffered from chronic daily headaches and they had not improved, despite physical therapy, oral painkillers, and activity restrictions. The injections worked very well for the majority of the patients. Nineteen months later, the majority (61 percent) of the patients had improved so that they experienced less than three headaches per week, rather than a headache every single day.

This type of treatment can be extremely effective, but localizing the correct joint is the key. This can be done with a careful clinical examination, but sometimes imaging of the spine or even using a diagnostic *electromyogram* (*EMG*), a test to measure nerve and muscle damage, can be helpful. Often, to increase the effectiveness of the joint block, doctors will perform the procedure under a fluoroscope—a special X-ray machine. This can increase the accuracy of the injection and therefore the amount of pain relief it provides.

to use massage therapy as a preventive measure to keep you from getting a headache, sometimes the pain can be seemingly rubbed out with a massage. This is especially true if you have chronic cervicogenic headaches that stem from tensed muscles in the neck and shoulder area. Massage therapy is also effective for patients with chronic tension-type headaches and migraines.

There are many licensed massage therapists and you may be able to get a prescription from your physician for massage therapy—although many health insurance companies still don't cover massage. If you have to pay for the therapy (assuming you can afford it), then consider it as important to your health (even if your insurance company doesn't); also, save your receipts in case you wish to claim a medical tax deduction. In addition, the therapist you use should have at least several years of experience. Most states license massage therapists, and they nearly always display their licenses prominently in their offices.

Chiropractic Adjustments Might Help

In some cases, an adjustment is in order. We're not talking about an attitude adjustment here, but instead we're referring to a chiropractic manipulation performed by an experienced chiropractor. Very simply put, a manipulation is an attempt to forcibly change one or more points in the spinal alignment, based on the chiropractor's analysis of your X-rays, your medical history, and the particular pain problem that you're suffering from.

Although many physicians are wary of chiropractors, some of our patients have experienced considerable pain relief after being treated by a chiropractor, which has transformed us into believers. Of course, the chiropractor should be someone who has been in business for at least five years, and who is experienced and knowledgeable in treating chronic neck pain.

Studies on whether chiropractic manipulations alone are effective are mixed: some studies indicate that patients with cervicogenic headaches do well with spinal manipulation, while others don't show a significant difference between patients who received manipulation or massage therapy. In fact, many chiropractors use both manipulation and massage therapy, so if you feel better, it can be impossible to determine which therapy helped you. Chiropractic care is recognized and approved by the American Medical Association, and it is routinely covered by most insurance companies. In many cases, this is an ideal option for the treatment of cervicogenic headaches.

Physical Therapy

Patients with chronic cervicogenic headaches may gain some resolution through physical therapy ordered by the doctor. The therapist teaches the patient basic ideas that are geared toward gaining both strength and mobility in the problem areas. These exercises should help you stretch and/or relax overly tense muscles. The exercises are also used to strengthen weak muscles and to help prevent future pain and problems. Many physical therapists also use heat to relax overstressed muscles, as well as massage therapy. They may also use electric stimulation ("e-stim") of the muscles to help patients with cervicogenic headaches, which we discuss more in Chapter 13.

Sometimes an overly aggressive physical therapist can cause you unnecessary pain. If the therapy is really hurting you, whatever is going on, tell the therapist you need her to stop now. There may be some pain involved in getting your muscles into better shape, but when the pain is sudden and severe, then something is wrong and you shouldn't continue with the therapy.

What Should Happen Before Starting Physical Therapy

Before physical therapy begins, the therapist should take a basic medical history from you, including when your headaches and neck pain (if you have neck pain) started, as well as what you've done, if anything, that helped you feel better. The therapist will also ask you about your career field (because some careers are more neck pain–inducing than others) and whether you have any other major illnesses.

Tailoring the Therapy to Your Needs

After gathering the information, the therapist will design a program for you, including exercises to perform during therapy as well as exercises that you can do at home. Some of the exercises you'll do with the therapist may use equipment while others are stretching exercises that you can perform without any special materials. Physical therapy sessions vary but generally last for about 30–60 minutes. The first session that you have with the therapist will probably be the longest, since it includes taking your history.

"Nexercises" That May Help

During physical therapy, you will probably be given some exercises focusing on the shoulder and neck area for relieving pain. We have also found that many patients benefit from performing some simple neck exercises ("nexercises") that we recommend, ranging from shoulder shrugs to what we call upward rows. (Of course it's important for you to always check with your doctor first before starting any exercise regimen, including ours.) You may even want to show your doctor these exercises to see if they would be safe for you to do. They don't take long, nearly anyone can accomplish them, and you don't need any equipment in order to do them. Doing these easy exercises for just a few minutes a day may mean major relief from your cervicogenic headaches or can possibly prevent them from occurring in the first place.

Don't underestimate the importance of a healthy neck. As we've discussed, chronic neck problems can often lead to cervicogenic headaches, whether the neck pain is related to arthritis, bad posture, sedentary behavior, traumas such as falls or whiplash, or it's from a combination of these causes or from other causes. But you *can* (and we think should) improve the stability and stamina of your neck and upper spine by performing many of our easy exercises, which can be done at work or home. We think you'll be surprised at the improved mobility, increased flexibility, and additional strength you'll enjoy from doing these exercises.

We include 17 neck exercises divided into three groups to perform over the next three weeks; and we hope they will reduce your neck pain and cervicogenic headaches. After the three-week period, continue doing the exercises from Week Three for at least a few times per week, in order to help you prevent cervicogenic headaches. These exercises were published in our book *Migraine: What Works!* (Prima Publishing, 1996) and are reproduced with permission here. We also include these and other exercises in our *Spinal Tips* videotape and booklet (Pain Management Consultants).

Week One Exercises

For this first week of exercises, do all of the exercises listed for Week One every day to improve flexibility and strength. After the first week, add the exercises in Week Two to those for Week One.

Exercise 1: Shoulder Shrugs (for flexibility and strength)

1. With arms relaxed at your side, lift your shoulders to your ears and circle back and down. (*Hint:* Squeeze your shoulder blades together on the rotation backward.)
2. Repeat 10 times.

Note: At no time during this exercise should your shoulders rotate forward.

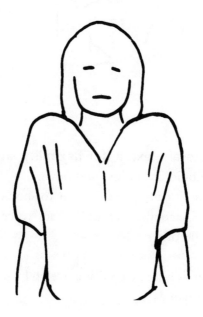

Exercise 2: Flexion and Extension
(for flexibility and strength)

1. Move your chin to chest and push shoulders down.
2. As you elevate your chin to ceiling, shrug your shoulders and hold for 1–2 seconds. To enhance the stretch in extended position, push your chin up.
3. Repeat 10 times in each direction.

Note: This exercise can be used as a stretch by holding each position for 10–20 seconds.

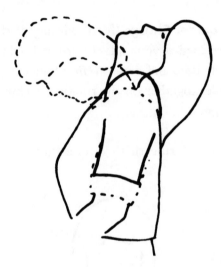

Exercise 3: Lateral Flexion (for flexibility and strength)

1. Shoulders should be relaxed and down.
2. Lift right ear to ceiling and left ear to shoulder.
3. Hold for 1–2 seconds, then move back to center.
4. Repeat on the other side.

Note: This exercise can be used as a stretch by holding each position for 10–20 seconds.

Exercise 4: Neck Rotation (for flexibility and strength)

1. Rotate your chin and ear to one side, and hold 1–2 seconds.
2. Look down at your shoulder, and move back to center.
3. Rotate in the opposite direction.
4. Repeat both rotations one more time.

Note: This exercise can be used as a stretch by holding each position for 10–20 seconds.

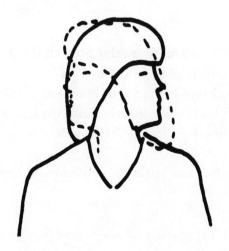

Exercise 5: Neck Retraction (for flexibility)

1. Squeeze your shoulder blades together.
2. Pull your head straight back, keeping jaw and eyes level.
3. Hold for 5–10 seconds and relax.
4. Repeat 10 times, trying to focus on proper posture during retraction.

Note: Do not drop or lift your chin during this exercise.

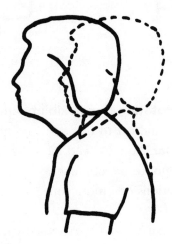

Exercise 6: Chest and Shoulder Stretch (for flexibility)

1. Squeeze your shoulder blades together.
2. Clasp your hands behind your body and extend your arms.
3. Gently lift hands and elbows toward the ceiling.
4. Stand tall and hold for 10–30 seconds.

Note: Hold the neck retracted while squeezing your shoulder blades together.

Modification: This exercise can also be done by placing your hands on a doorway and passing the torso through the entrance.

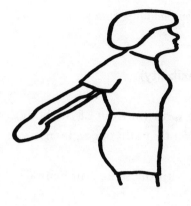

Week Two

Continue working on building your strength and flexibility by doing this next group of exercises, every day.

Exercise 7: Shoulder Retraction (for strength)

1. With your fingers touching the ears and elbows up, pinch your shoulder blades together (as you do this, your elbows will move back).
2. Hold for 5 seconds and release shoulder blades. Do not pull or push the neck.

Note: Hold the neck retracted (see Exercise 5: Neck Retraction) while squeezing the shoulder blades together.

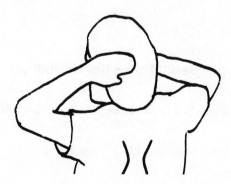

Modification: If it is painful to have your hands behind your ears, then place your hands on your shoulders.

Exercise 8: Neck Stretch (for flexibility)

1. Lift your right ear to ceiling.
2. Grasp your right arm above the wrist (in front of the body) and drop your shoulder as you gently pull your right arm down.
3. Hold for 10 seconds and repeat with the same arm behind the back.
4. Repeat to the other side.

Note: To enhance this stretch, rotate the chin up and down.

Exercise 9: Upper Back Stretch (for flexibility)
First Stage:

1. Clasp hands together in front of the body with both arms extended.
2. Gently pull your shoulder blades apart and drop your chin to your chest.
3. Hold for 10–30 seconds.

Second Stage:

1. Sit in a chair, cross your arms, and grab the armrests.
2. Move your chin to your chest as you open your shoulder blades.

Exercise 10: Prone Retraction (for flexibility)

1. Lie on the corner of a bed, face down, head and neck relaxed.
2. With your arms bent and elbows raised, squeeze your shoulder blades together, raising the elbows, and hold for 5 seconds.
3. Build up to holding for 15 seconds.
4. Repeat 5 times, and then repeat Exercise 9.

Note: Place a pillow under your hips for support.

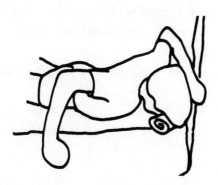

Week Three

For the third week, you'll be doing some more challenging exercises and stretches to really work on building strength.

Exercise 11: Abdominal Crunches (for strength)

1. Lie on your back with your knees bent and feet flat on the floor.
2. With hands at your side, lift your head and shoulders off the floor, moving hands either toward your ankles or knees as you lift.
3. Repeat this exercise 5 times.

Note: Your head should be in a rigid position (pretend to have an apple between your chin and chest while lifting).

Note: It is normal for the neck muscles to become fatigued.

Exercise 12: Arm Lifts (for strength)

1. Lie on the corner of a bed facedown, with your head and neck relaxed.
2. Extend arms over your head and raise your arms toward the ceiling.
3. Hold for 2–5 seconds, increasing to 15 seconds over time.
4. Repeat 5 times, and then repeat flexibility Exercises 6 and 9.

Note: Place a pillow under your hips for support.

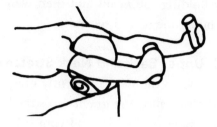

Exercise 13: Stabilization of Shoulder Girdle (for strength)

1. Lie on the corner of a bed face down. Relax your head and neck.

Note: Place a pillow under your hips for support.

2. With arms extended out to the side, squeeze your shoulder blades together and raise both arms toward the ceiling.
3. Hold for 5–10 seconds.
4. Build up to holding for 20 seconds and repeat flexibility Exercise 9.

Note: This exercise will become easier over time. It can be advanced by holding soup cans and then weights. In that case, reduce your hold time to 1–3 seconds.

Exercise 14: Upper Back and Neck Stretch (for flexibility)

1. Tilt your head to the side, and gently grasp the side of your head (at the ear) allowing gravity to stretch the muscles.
2. Place your opposite hand behind your back and hold for 10–20 seconds.

Note: Do not pull on your head and neck!

Exercise 15: Shoulder Reach (for strength)

1. Lie on your back with your arms extended toward the ceiling.
2. Attempt to open your shoulder blades as you push your arms straight up to the ceiling. (Keep your back against the floor and elbows straight.)
3. Hold for 5 seconds.
4. Build up to 15 seconds and repeat flexibility Exercise 6.

Exercise 17: Upward Row (for strength)

1. Stand tall with your shoulder blades squeezing together.
2. Hold a towel with both hands in front of your body, palms facing toward the body.
3. Leading with the elbows, lift both hands to the chin and hold; squeezing your shoulder blades together in this position.
4. Repeat stretches 8 and 14.

Note: At the end of the exercise, your elbows should be higher than your ears and wrists.

Modification: Once this movement becomes familiar, you can add 1–5 pound weights and repeat 10–20 times.

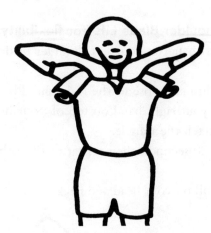

Additional At-Home Therapies That Can Help with Pain

In addition to medications, injections, physical therapy, and exercises, some patients incorporate additional at-home therapies into their treatment program. However, we recommend talking to

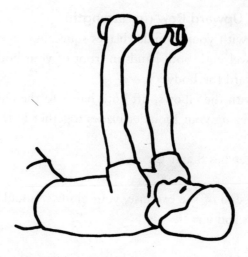

Exercise 16: Shoulder Blade Lift (for flexibility)

1. Place your left hand on your left shoulder blade, elevating your elbow.
2. Move your chin and nose to the right shoulder.
3. Gently place your right hand on top of your head, allowi gravity to stretch the muscle.
4. Hold for 10–20 seconds, then repeat to the other side.

Note: Do not pull on your head and neck.

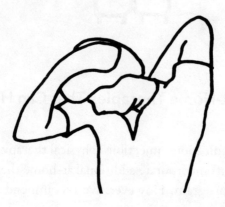

your doctor first before using any of these additional treatments, exercises, devices, or other home remedies.

Traction Devices

Most patients with cervicogenic headaches are not put into traction in the hospital because it is unnecessary and extremely expensive. Traction is a therapy that uses a combination of pulleys and levers to exert extra force upon the area that is being treated. Although you probably won't receive in-patient traction, you may, however, benefit from an at-home cervical traction device. These items are available at most medical supply stores and can also be ordered online.

Traction devices vary in how they're set up, and many of them use weights that you can connect to a door or a closet opening. When you set up the device for the first time, for the sake of safety, make sure that another adult is with you; and also check that you can readily release yourself from the device without any assistance. **Do *not* use this device on a child with neck pain and/or cervicogenic headaches.** They are designed for the weight of an adult.

Basically, nearly all of these devices involve you sitting down while your head is fitted inside a cervical collar. You then press a button or some other device that enables your head and neck to be pulled and stretched upwards. You may be thinking of the torture rack used in the Inquisition; but in this case, the "rack" is a good thing because it's used to relieve your pain by stretching your overstrained muscles, rather than inflicting pain upon you.

The first time you use such a device you may worry that you could end up causing harm or even accidentally hanging yourself. The device would not hold your entire weight (so you can't hang yourself); and you should have no other problems if you carefully follow the directions provided with the device, as well as the directions that you receive from your doctor. We generally advise our patients to start low and go slow. That is, we usually recommend 10 pounds of weight for 8–10 minutes, one to two times per day. When patients get more comfortable, we let them increase the time and the weight load.

Generally, you'll use the traction device for 5 or 10 minutes at a time and you may use it daily or on another schedule, depending on your doctor's instructions. You may notice relief after several sessions or it may take longer. Some people who incorporate the traction device into their daily routine are able to avert most of their cervicogenic headaches.

Getting Hot Under the Collar with Heating Cervical Collars

Although most doctors treating cervicogenic headaches no longer rely on soft cervical collars, which are devices that fit around your neck and encourage immobility, there's a new type of heated cervical collar that may offer significant pain relief to patients with cervicogenic headaches. These devices generate penetrating heat that can help to relax your aching and taut neck muscles. With your neck muscles relaxed, the cervicogenic headache is then averted.

Some cervical collars are heated up in your microwave oven, while others rely upon packets that are self-heating and then fit in an inside pocket of the collar. The pain relief you'll gain is only temporary, but when you're hurting a lot, even a brief respite from pain is well worth it.

Of course you could use a heating pad instead of a heated cervical collar, but with the heating pad you'd need to lie down on the pad to gain the benefit, whereas with the heated collars, you can move about while you're at home or work.

Surgical Interventions

Some patients with severe chronic cervicogenic headaches have been treated with minor or major surgical procedures, such as the *percutaneous radiofrequency neurotomy*, a procedure that uses radiofrequency waves to degrade the offending nerve. If you have degenerative disk disease, and bulging disks are causing pain, surgery may be in order. In extreme cases, a spinal fusion is recommended.

The Radiofrequency Neurotomy

In the radiofrequency neurotomy procedure, the nerve that is causing your pain is directly addressed by affecting the nerve's blood supply. The physician anesthetizes the target nerve that he has already determined is the key pain generator. The nerve to be treated is typically first injected with lidocaine, and then radiofrequency waves are directed at the nerve to cut off its blood supply and your pain.

In one study of 30 patients with chronic cervicogenic headaches, described in 2004 in *Pain News*, a newsletter from the American Association of Neurological Surgeons, the researchers found that this procedure reduced the average number of headaches from 6.2 days per week to 2.8 days weekly. It also reduced the amount of painkillers that patients needed by an average of 70 percent, a dramatic reduction.

Spinal Fusion

When the pain is continuous, and especially if the disks have herniated, the doctor may recommend a spinal fusion. With a spinal fusion, which is rarely needed in patients with cervicogenic headaches, the surgeon removes the disk that is causing the severe pain. Without the disk, the bones will eventually fuse together. Often the neurosurgeon will use devices like screws, plates, or bone material to assist in the fusion.

The spinal fusion is a very complex procedure with an extended and painful recovery period of at least several months, and this procedure should be performed only by an experienced neurosurgeon or an orthopedic surgeon. It should never be undergone without a great deal of thought beforehand. By definition, with any fusion there is some loss of function of the neck, particularly the range of motion. That is another reason why this procedure should only be used as a final option.

Now that you have explored the various treatment options for cervicogenic headaches, you can take a look at the last chapter in this section, where we discuss strategies and steps you can take in order to protect your neck and spine and prevent these headaches from occurring.

CHAPTER 6

What You Can Do to Prevent Neck Headaches

In the last chapter, we talked about medical treatments and exercises that are effective in helping patients cope with their cervicogenic headaches. But wouldn't it be great to avoid getting these headaches in the first place? This chapter is about practical recommendations to help you *prevent* your chronic neck headaches from either starting or—if you already have the early onset of a headache—from getting even worse. Of course sometimes headaches will occur anyway, even if you carefully follow our good ideas. So don't expect a complete remission forever from all your cervicogenic headaches; but we think that you'll find that they're less frequent and less intense when you carry out our suggestions.

A major part of prevention includes considering what you're doing now (or *not* doing) and changing some patterns that you may be displaying (but weren't aware of), both at work and at home. These types of changes include no longer doing such things as awkwardly cradling the phone between your head and shoulder as you talk for minutes or hours. This can really build up tension in your neck muscles, and it can also lead to painful headaches.

We also have suggestions for people who spend a great deal of time on the computer, which can be a headache-inducing activity, if you're not careful. In addition, we talk about a group that many people don't stop to consider: mothers who have babies and/or small children. These mothers often develop neck pain and cervicogenic headaches from the constant lifting and carrying around of their offspring. Of course we're not recommending that you leave your baby in her crib all the time, but we do offer other ideas for your consideration.

It's also a good idea to consider your basic headache triggers, as discussed in Chapter 3. Many people with cervicogenic headaches are very sensitive to intense light and loud noise, which may trigger a headache or greatly worsen a headache that's already started.

Analyze Your Phone Style (Neck Craning Versus Headset)

How many people do you see walking around with their cell phones cradled between their head and neck, with their head contorted oddly to the side? And how many people assume this position either at home or at work on their regular phones? It's an extremely common sight, and many of these people are setting themselves up for neck pain and for developing or worsening cervicogenic headaches.

To find out if you exhibit this type of behavior, pick up a phone and then assume your normal talking position. Not the way you think we want you to position yourself, but the way you really *do* hold the phone. Now, hold that position for at least three minutes. Think about how your neck feels, as well as your shoulders. Are they tense? Does your neck or your shoulder hurt? We're only asking you to hold this position for a few minutes, but many people spend at least an hour a day on the phone, with one shoulder hunched all the way up to their ear, so high it's like an extra earring.

Now, while you stay in this position, pretend you're talking on the phone and look at yourself in the mirror. Is your head at a very awkward angle? Does one shoulder stick up while the other is relaxed? Just observing yourself in the mirror can show you how common telephone positions can create chronic neck pain, especially if you already have another medical problem like arthritis, whiplash, or degenerative disk disease. However, even if you don't have any of these problems, awkward phone positions can be headache-inducing.

So what should you do? You can purchase inexpensive telephone headsets, so that you can speak freely without having to contort your body to communicate with your fellow workers, family members, or friends. This will also allow you to multitask with your now liberated hands. Another idea is that you can send more e-mails to communicate with people. (An added bonus is that e-mails give you a written record of what is said, while the essence of phone conversations can be misunderstood or forgotten.)

When you have to use your cell phone, stand or sit normally and just hold the device to your ear—without attempting to balance it. There are also headsets available for cell phones, so if you have long cell phone conversations, you should definitely consider a headset. In some states and cities (for example, New York City), it's against the law *not* to use a headset when talking on a cell phone in your car. (For your own safety, however, we advise against holding cell phone conversations when you're driving, even when it's lawful behavior.) If you are alone at home, your office, or another location, you can also use the speaker phone that's available on many cell phones, so that you can hear easily and respond.

Consider the Items You Carry with You

It doesn't occur to most people, but if you're like many others, every day you may be lugging around as much as 15 or 20 extra pounds in the form of a purse, briefcase, or backpack, which is causing a severe strain and pain in your neck and your head. This lifestyle error could be at least part of the reason for your chronic cervicogenic headaches.

If you're a woman, we're betting that your purse is a lot heavier than you realize. And whether you're a man or a woman, the briefcase can become extremely unwieldy too. Here's what we recommend:

- Weigh your purse or briefcase to get a clear understanding of what you are actually carrying around.
- Get rid of all the extra change in your purse or briefcase. Those coins can get pretty heavy in a matter of days. Keep only a few dollars worth, at most, and turn the rest in for paper money at the bank.
- Consider replacing your current heavy cell phone with a newer and lighter version.
- Clean out your purse or briefcase at least weekly so you'll avoid toting around unnecessary extra paper and other items that can add up quickly to too many pounds.
- Avoid wearing heavy jewelry around your neck.
- If you have a baby, avoid using sling devices that go around your neck. (They're very bad for people with chronic neck pain—and everyone else.)

Your Lifting Strategy: Some Changes Might Be in Order

People with chronic neck headaches should also be careful about how much weight they lift (in general, more than 30 pounds is probably too much for the average person with neck pain), and also *how* they lift items. Avoid lifting heavy items all the way up to your shoulders; instead, keep them at your center of gravity, near the waistline, as much as possible. Better yet, don't lift heavy items if you can avoid doing so! It's bad for your neck and the rest of your spine. When you need to lift something, here's what we recommend:

- Keep the item that you're lifting close to your body rather than held at arm's length. This will make the weight easier to carry.

- Stand close to the item before you lift it, rather than reaching for it as you lift it.
- When lifting the object, bend your knees and hips, rather than leaning over and arching your back to lift the item.
- It may be easier to lift an item off the floor when you have one foot in front of the other, rather than having your feet planted exactly together.

Your Office Chair: Is It Pain-Free?

If you work in an office, does your chair have arms? If not, you'll need to trade it in for a new chair that's less headache-inducing. An ergonomically friendly chair can translate into fewer headaches for many people. Your feet should fit firmly and comfortably on the floor, without your knees sticking up like a grasshopper. (Yes, all these tips are related to neck pain. The more contorted that your head and body is, the more likely you are to have neck pain; and neck pain often leads to cervicogenic headaches.)

It's best to have an adjustable chair, especially if you use a computer frequently in your work. In that case, you need to be sitting so that the monitor is about 20–26 inches directly in front of you. The center of the computer monitor should be about 4–9 inches below where you normally look when you stare straight ahead. However, if you wear bifocals, as many people do, then the situation is different. In that case, the bottom of your glasses should be where you should do your centering from, such that if you drew a straight line from the bottom of your glasses to the computer, that line would be straight ahead to the center of your computer. If it's not, then adjust your chair or your computer monitor so that you're positioned correctly.

Make sure your chair has casters so you can roll around. Too many people fail to move in their chairs, and casters encourage more movement. (You may need to purchase a mat to go under the chair, to avoid damaging your carpet.) Your chair should have five casters because the five-point positioning is best for stability and safety. You may also wish to use a footrest to attain a better position.

What About Your Computer? Ideas for Improvement

In Chapter 3, we talked about computer vision syndrome and how constantly staring at your computer can be harmful to your eyes and lead to chronic headaches. In this chapter, we get into some basics on making your computer experience significantly more neck- and head-friendly.

The Position of Your Computer Monitor, Your Keyboard, and Mouse

Are you craning or straining your neck to read what's on your computer monitor? You may be too far away or too close. You may also need glasses or new glasses, so be sure that you get a vision check every year.

Is your keyboard and/or your mouse positioned so that you have to lift your shoulders or elbows up to use them? If so, this is bad for your neck and shoulders, according to James Sheedy, a clinical professor at the University of California at Berkeley and an expert in computer ergonomics. In his booklet, *ErgoKit: Ergonomic Solutions for Comfortable Computing*, Sheedy says the keyboard and mouse must be either at or a little lower than your elbows in a relaxed position. If the keyboard or mouse is too high, then you could develop aches and pains in your shoulders, neck, and back. An adjustable keyboard tray may be the right answer for you. Alternatively, you could raise your chair up. Sheedy also notes that if your monitor is too high or low, this can cause pain in the neck and shoulders. Additional adaptive devices, such as a wrist pad for the keyboard and a mouse pad with a wrist support can be very helpful. A wireless mouse may also make it easier for some people to move about a bit more freely and more frequently.

Here's an odd-sounding idea. Consider moving your mouse from one side to the other. If you're a righty, move it to the left and lefties, move right. It'll feel a little strange at first, but if you do this for a day or so, you may find that you've relaxed your shoulder and neck.

Take Breaks from Work

Too many people sit almost like statues while they work on their computers. Take a break at least once every hour. Here's an idea for one of your breaks: drop your hands off the keyboard and notice any tension in your neck. You may realize that you've been hunching up your shoulders while you type. If you're aware of a habit like this, it's easier to break it. Doing shoulder shrugs and neck exercises during your work breaks may have a dramatic impact on reducing your headache symptoms.

Use a Document Holder

Do you constantly look back and forth from the computer monitor to papers on your desk or table? This can cause considerable neck pain over weeks. (Or years!) Consider purchasing an inexpensive document holder (sold at most office-supply stores or at computer stores) that you can site at the same level of your monitor and to one side. Then you can glance from the screen to the holder, without needing to bob your head up and down to do your work. Maybe your document holder can't hold all the papers you need, but you can probably only work on 15–20 sheets in a reasonable time interval, so put those papers up on the holder. When you're done with them, hang up the next batch.

Other Headache-Inducing Issues at Home

In addition to the phone and your computer, there are also other common household items that may induce or worsen your cervicogenic headache problem. For example, consider your vacuum cleaner. Is it very heavy and do you hunch over when you use it? Think about getting a lightweight and more ergonomically friendly vacuum cleaner. One of our patients even went so far as to buy a robotic vacuum cleaner! Yes, these alternatives could be expensive, but so are numerous visits to your doctor, medications, trigger injections, and so forth.

What about your bed? If you sleep with giant fluffy pillows in a nice soft bed, you could be courting disaster in the form of neck aches as well as back pain. Instead, consider sleeping with no pillows on a firm bed, or buy a firmer pillow with good neck support.

Experts advise that if you have neck pain (or if you have cervicogenic headaches, which inevitably stem from a neck problem), then you shouldn't sleep on your stomach. It places far too much stress on the neck. Instead, sleep on your back or on your side. Some of our patients have found that using a body pillow can help them with their positioning in bed; and this helps to take the stress off of the entire spine.

Some Suggestions for Moms with Babies and Small Children

One much-ignored group of people at risk for developing cervicogenic headaches is mothers with babies and small children. The constant lifting and carrying of wiggling children who may weigh up to 30 pounds or more can be a major strain on the neck. We have some preventive ideas for these mothers. (And our ideas also work well for fathers who are the primary caregivers.)

First, instead of lugging a heavy diaper bag around with you everywhere you go, we recommend placing the diaper bag on a rolling cart like the ones that flight attendants use. This will reduce the strain on your body and the heavy lifting. We also recommend that you consider using two smaller bags to carry your baby paraphernalia, rather than trying to stuff everything that you've got into one large bag. It may seem a little inconvenient, but your body will appreciate this courtesy!

It's a good idea to vary your baby caretaking positions so that you're not constantly holding the baby. Use the infant seat, stroller, and playpen rather than carrying your baby or toddler everywhere. Don't worry, you'll still be able to bond with your child just fine even when you don't constantly carry her everywhere.

When you change your baby, use a changing table or place her somewhere that is at your waist level, so that you don't have to contort your body to do diaper duty. Having all of the changing items at hand and at the appropriate level can reduce your bending and twisting. If you use a changing table and the phone rings, take her with you or put her in her crib before answering, or let the answering machine pick it up. Many accidents occur with even tiny babies falling from changing tables.

When you take the baby in or out of the crib, make sure to lower the rails so that you don't have to strain to get her. Trying to pull her over the extended crib rails can place a great deal of stress on your neck—not to mention on the baby!

Here's one item we urge new moms to avoid altogether, especially when they have chronic neck pain. This is the sling-type infant carrier that you hang around your neck, sort of like a feedbag hung around a horse's neck. (But the horse is on four feet and you're walking erectly; thus, the pressure from this position is much worse for you than it is for the horse. We thought we'd mention this, in case any animal-loving readers started worrying about horses.) The weight of the baby, even when she's only 15 pounds or so, can be very damaging to your neck. Do not strap one of these on yourself! Instead, carry her in your arms or put her in the stroller or a baby carriage. Or let your spouse or partner carry her for a while. We point out to our patients a simple physics lesson—that is, it is not just the weight of your baby but rather the weight multiplied by the distance from the ground multiplied by the force of gravity that is actually the force being generated around your neck!

Consider the Effects of Light and Sounds

In Chapter 3, we talked about the fact that many people with cervicogenic headaches are very sensitive to bright light and loud noise. Another problem is that people can develop cervicogenic headaches from riding in cars. This section is about dealing with these sensitivities. Even if you think you're not affected by these problems, try out our suggestions to see if they help you. You might be surprised at the improvements that occur.

Bright Lights

Intense sunlight or artificial light can be bothersome to many people with cervicogenic headaches. You can't live in a cave, but you can take some preventive actions. For example, wear sunglasses outside or buy prescription glasses that darken under bright lights. When you go to the beach, limit your sun exposure and sit under an umbrella after a certain time—say, after 30 or more minutes have passed.

Check your windows. Do you sit in an area that has a lot of glare from the sun? Move elsewhere or put up blinds or heavy curtains for when the sun is overly bright. It isn't crazy to wear sunglasses in the house if you need to in order to avoid sunlight glare.

Avoid using old fluorescent lights in your home. If they are used at work, ask your supervisor to use the newer fluorescents, which are less prone to flickering and are also much less headache-inducing.

Some people have a problem with bright light reflecting off their computer monitors. You could relocate your computer to a darker place at home or work. Or you could consider buying an antiglare screen for your computer screen. Another idea is to wear a visor while you're using the computer. This is also a good idea if bright lights in the room are bothering you.

Loud Noise

If you can't hear yourself think because of the cacophony around you, this is a bad situation and can lead to headaches for many people prone to cervicogenic headaches. If you can't turn off the noise or convince everyone to be quiet, consider using earplugs. A white-noise generator (there are inexpensive ones available) to help you block the loud noises emanating from others—if you can't induce them to silence—may be the thing you need. It's also probably best if you don't get a job operating a jackhammer or other loud equipment if noise is a headache trigger!

Driving in Cars

If you find that driving a car (or even riding in a car) is headache-inducing or greatly worsens your headaches, then you may need to rethink a long commute to the office. Of course you can also consider taking preventive medications such as Topamax (topiramate) (discussed in Chapter 10) that may help to prevent headaches from occurring. (If you're a long-haul truck driver, you may need to rethink your choice of occupation.)

At the very least, check your position in the vehicle to see if you are sitting in an ergonomically correct fashion. Are your knees resting slightly higher than your hips? Are you comfortable with your hands on the steering wheel, with a slight bend at the elbows? These are just a few things to check if you are going to be in your vehicle for any extended length of time.

We hope these suggestions help you on the road to lessening or preventing your cervicogenic headaches. Read on to the next section to find more information about other types of chronic headaches; or if you know that you suffer from cervicogenic headaches, flip to the last section for more detailed information on how to work with your doctor for better treatment.

Migraines and Other Chronic Severe Headaches

In this section, we cover other chronic headaches besides the cervicogenic headache. In one chapter, we provide an in-depth look at migraines, while in other chapters we zero in on cluster headaches, tension-type headaches, occipital neuralgia headaches, combination headaches, sinus headaches, rebound headaches, and emergency headaches. You'll also find out about the medical problems that sometimes cause chronic headaches, such as thyroid disease and hypertension.

CHAPTER 7

The Migraine

Sometimes called a "sick headache" or a "blinding headache," the migraine almost always causes severe head pain, driving sufferers into their bedrooms to hide with their pain that's so overwhelming that they are in a sensory overload. Sunlight or even a minor sound can supersize the headache pain to an agonizingly higher level, and because of this, the migraine sufferer usually wants people to whisper any comments to her while she lies very still in a dark room. Better yet, they should leave her alone altogether until the headache subsides.

Migraines are extremely common, and if you suffer from them, you're definitely not alone. But at the risk of sounding silly, this is actually a good time for people with migraines, because there are many effective medications and treatments available today that migraineurs in the past would have been thrilled to have access to. If you could somehow go back in time to 20 or more years ago, the migraine sufferers you'd talk to would find it impossible to believe that a little pill taken at the onset of a migraine could stop it cold—or that other medications or treatments such as Botox injections could markedly decrease the frequency and severity of migraines in many people. They would be amazed to learn that identifying your personal headache triggers is a major step to thwarting migraines from occurring in the first place. Now, fast forward to today, when we *do* have many good

Who Gets Migraines?

An estimated 28 million adults in the United States suffer from migraines. Most sufferers are female (about 18 percent of the female adults), but about 6 percent of males in the United States suffer from migraines. In general, migraines most commonly occur among people between the ages of 25 and 55 years old, although patients who are both younger and older may also suffer from this headache type.

Migraines are a global problem. In a study of 5,553 adults in the United States, France, Germany, Italy, and the United Kingdom, reported in a 2003 issue of *Headache*, researchers found that the percentage of the population with migraines was highest in Italy (12 percent), followed by the United States and Germany (11 percent each), the United Kingdom (7 percent), and France (5 percent). (It's unknown what accounts for the difference in migraine incidence in different countries.) The researchers also found that about half of the respondents with migraine symptoms hadn't sought out the help of a physician, relying instead on over-the-counter remedies to treat their severe headaches.

Only about 10 percent of the migraineurs in this study had been prescribed triptan drugs (discussed more in Chapter 10), which are medications that are specific for treating migraines. The highest percentage (19 percent) of patients who were using triptans was in the United States, while the lowest (3 percent) was in Italy. Many experts, including us, are concerned that triptans are woefully underprescribed, and this study as well as others backs up our concern.

ways to treat and prevent migraines, and when medical researchers will continue to make even more medical breakthroughs. Looking at it this way, it seems less strange to say that now is a good time to suffer from migraines.

But migraines are still terrible headaches, and if you or someone you care about experiences recurrent migraines, this chapter is important for you. We talk about who primarily suffers from migraines (what doctors call the "epidemiology" of migraines), theories on why migraines occur, and why they are often misdiagnosed as sinus headaches. We also cover migraine symptoms and what you can do about your migraines. The menstrual migraine, a problem experienced by the majority of women with migraines, is another topic we discuss in this chapter.

Migraines Are Often Misdiagnosed as Other Headaches

Many patients are not diagnosed with migraines for years, and instead, they are diagnosed with other forms of headaches, such as sinus headaches or tension-type headaches; or they are not diagnosed at all.

In a study conducted in 1999, the American Migraine Study II, more than half (52 percent) of individuals with migraine symptoms had *not* been diagnosed with migraines. A more recent study, reported in 2004 in *Headache*, based on 1,203 patients in 15 countries (including the United States), showed a somewhat better diagnostic record. In considering all patients, about 25 percent who probably had migraines, based on their headache diaries, had not been diagnosed with migraines by their physicians. This is still too many undiagnosed migraine patients, but it's a better finding than in the American Migraine Study II.

Migraine Is Often Misdiagnosed as Sinus Headache

Sometimes patients who suffer from chronic migraines are misdiagnosed with sinus headaches. Migraine patients may show up in the doctor's office with a runny nose and tearing eyes, which are key reasons for this misdiagnosis. But there's other common ground between migraines and sinus headaches that can sometimes mislead the doctor. For example, both migraines and sinus headaches may be triggered by weather changes, such as snowy or rainy weather. It's also true that often the pain of migraines and sinus headaches occurs in the same area of the head. However, patients who really do have sinusitis also have a fever (and most migraineurs are not feverish), and X-rays of their heads will show a sinus blockage (a finding you won't see in a patient with migraine).

Apparently sinus headaches may be misdiagnosed even more frequently than we and many other doctors ever imagined. In a study reported in a 2004 issue of *Archives of Internal Medicine*, the researchers made a shocking finding: 88 percent of nearly 3,000 patients who were previously diagnosed with sinusitis really had migraines rather than sinus headaches, a very daunting percentage. What confused both the patients and their doctors was the location of the headache (around and below the eyes as well as at the cheeks), the nasal congestion, the watery eyes, and the runny nose that accompanied their headaches.

Misdiagnosis as Migraine When It's Another Headache Type

In addition to migraines being incorrectly diagnosed as sinus headaches, there's another type of headache misdiagnosis that sometimes occurs. As we discussed in the chapters in Part II, some people are diagnosed with migraines when they really have another type of headache—particularly in the case of cervicogenic headaches.

Symptoms of Migraine Headaches

The classic symptoms of a migraine headache are the following, although you may have some and not all of them:

- Head pain
- Nausea and vomiting
- Sensitivity to light and sound
- Coldlike symptoms
- Prodrome and/or aura
- Significantly below-normal functioning (at work and at home) when the headache hits

Head Pain

The most common symptom of a migraine is excruciatingly severe head pain. Some patients say that on a scale of 1 to 10, a migraine is about a 50 (because it's so far beyond the normal everyday pain that most people are used to). However, once in a while patients have migraines with other symptoms, but minus the headache pain.

When head pain does occur, which is nearly always, the pain is often a one-sided pain (unilateral), although sometimes the pain may switch from one side of the head to the other, for no apparent reason. This rarely happens in the same headache event; rather, the location can switch sides from headache to headache. In about a third of all migraine cases, the pain may occur simultaneously on both sides of the head. Of all the symptoms of migraine, the head pain is usually the most distressing to patients. This pain may last from several hours to as long as several days before it abates—unless the right medication is taken.

Nausea and Vomiting

Many people with chronic migraines suffer from nausea and vomiting. Sometimes they feel better after vomiting and other times, they feel just as bad as beforehand. If you find that you can't keep your headache medication down because of a problem with nausea and vomiting, be sure to ask your doctor for antinausea medicine, also known as an *antiemetic*. Often these drugs can be inserted rectally. This may sound a little disgusting to you, but do you want the nausea to end? Then be very grateful for rectal suppositories! They are also quite sedating—another good thing, as sleep can often bring relief from pain.

Sensitivity to Light and Sound

As we discussed in Chapter 3 on headache triggers, intense light and loud noise are major triggers for many people with migraines; and they also worsen a migraine once it's already started. A sensitivity to light is often called *photophobia*, while a sensitivity to noise is called *phonophobia*. Despite how these words sound, people who are sensitive to bright light or loud noise aren't actually afraid of these things, but instead they cause them intense pain. So this kind of "phobia" is nothing like a phobia/fear of snakes, spiders, or other intense fears, despite the nomenclature.

Coldlike Symptoms

As mentioned earlier, because many migraine sufferers experience watery eyes and runny noses, these headaches are often misdiagnosed as sinus headaches. However, sinus medication won't help you, if and when your problem is a migraine. It may dry out your sinuses and the over-the-counter medication in most cold medications (such as Tylenol) may give you very mild relief. But that is all. You need migraine medication to treat a migraine headache.

The Prodrome and the Migraine "Aura"

Although sometimes migraines just appear out of nowhere, they don't always start out that way. Sometimes there's an advance warning called a *prodrome*, which may be followed by another form of advance warning called an *aura*. Or sometimes there's no prodrome and there is an aura, or there is a prodrome and no aura occurs.

What's a prodrome? It's often a generalized feeling of being somehow "off." Patients may experience a vague feeling of unrest or uneasiness for several hours or even days before they get a migraine. Many people with prodromes have difficulty explaining how the prodrome feels, and therefore they shrug it off. Many patients are reluctant to talk about these feelings, concerned that others will think them mentally unbalanced, not realizing that the prodrome is actually a common headache alert.

Some people experience sleepiness or even euphoria in the prodrome period, while others become more acutely sensitive to bright lights and/or loud noises or even odors. Many of our patients describe difficulty with concentration as one sign of their prodrome.

Prodromes and auras are different. The migraine prodrome isn't as specific as an aura, which is a sensory experience such as seeing jagged lines in front of your eyes or smelling something that isn't there.

Patients with Prodromes. Some studies have indicated that patients who experience prodromes differ from those who don't have them. In a study of 893 patients with migraines, reported in a 2004 issue of *Headache*, researchers found that about one-third of the subjects had prodrome symptoms. They also found that patients with prodrome had more headache triggers than those without them; and when the prodrome subjects did experience a migraine aura as well, it lasted longer than among patients without them. In addition, the headaches among the patients with prodromes lasted longer and responded slower to triptan medications. Patients with prodromes also had more cases of such symptoms as nausea, runny nose, and tearing of the eyes.

When the headache pain subsided, the prodrome patients had a greater prevalence of what doctors refer to as postprodrome syndrome. This phenomenon, if it happens, is characterized primarily by severe fatigue (which is common) and tenderness in the scalp area. Some patients can't eat in the postprodrome period.

Like a bad joke, the good news about prodromes is that you *know* a migraine is coming and you can get ready. The bad news about prodromes is pretty much the same thing—you know a headache's on the way. However, if you take your migraine medication during the prodrome phase, you may be able to abort the headache altogether. Or, if you still get a headache, then taking medication early on for an acute migraine can make the headache less intense. Please note that far too many people delay *too long* in taking their medication, thinking that maybe it'll go away, or that maybe they just need to rest, or all sorts of other rationalizations. Don't make this mistake!

What You Need to Know About Migraine Auras. Auras, which are experienced by about 20 percent of migraine patients, are very different from prodromes. Migraine auras are sensory experiences that—similar to prodromes—signal that a migraine is on its way, so watch out! Some auras can be disturbing, such as seeing jagged lines like thunder bolts in front of your eyes that you know aren't really there. Some patients smell a strange odor when no one else can smell it. Others experience *paresthesias* (pins and needles) or they have temporary trouble with their vision. Still others may have distortions of their hearing to the point of having difficulty carrying on a conversation.

The migraine aura is usually briefer than the prodrome, and it may last from about 5 or 10 minutes to as long as an hour or so. Then the headache pain itself will hit, which is the next headache stage.

Significantly Suboptimal Functioning

Most patients in the agonizing throes of a migraine are at below-normal levels of performance in all areas of functioning from what is normal for them. They usually cannot work and are at a mental impasse until the pain passes. It's almost as if people in the midst of a migraine lose about 20 or so IQ points. They really didn't lose their intelligence; but instead, their ability to listen, analyze, and respond is severely impaired—which shows them at a marked disadvantage both at work and at home.

Possible Causes of Migraines

Physicians have argued for years over what causes migraines, whether it's an imbalance of neurochemicals (such as serotonin), a problem with the structure of the brain, genetic factors, or many other causes or combination of causes. At the present time, many experts believe that genes, migraine triggers, and a few other causes are the primary culprits generating migraines. In the case of the menstrual migraine, however, the cause is hormonal.

It's Often Genetic

Many studies have shown a genetic aspect of migraine headaches. For example, several studies of family members who suffer from migraines have found a common mutation in the CACNA1A gene, especially among patients who have migraine with aura. Other studies have found an involvement of chromosome 19p in migraine patients both with and without aura. The dopamine D2 receptor gene has been linked to migraine with aura; and the serotonin transporter gene has been tied to both migraine with and migraine without aura.

Continued research is likely to yield further genetic information. However, since we can't alter the genes that are already encoded into our bodies (at least, not yet!), it's not really useful information for most consumers. The value of knowing that migraines may have a genetic link occurs when someone in the family develops headaches, and this information can be shared with a physician.

For example, if you and your sibling have both suffered from migraines for years, and your teenage daughter starts getting headaches, the doctor will be interested to learn that migraines run in the family. She'll run the appropriate tests and do a thorough examination, but the knowledge that migraine was a problem in other family members is another valued piece of the diagnostic puzzle for her.

In addition, sometimes medications that work well in one family member with a problem will also help another family member. For example, if you suffer from migraines and respond well to Imitrex (sumatriptan), make sure to tell that to the doctor, as she will probably try Imitrex on your daughter, too, to see if she responds well. However, sometimes close family members do not respond well to the same medications. Also, keep in mind that if Imitrex hasn't worked for you (or your daughter), the doctor may try another triptan medication. (Often if one triptan doesn't work, another one will be effective.)

Migraine Triggers

Migraine triggers definitely play a major role in migraine headaches. As a quick review from Chapter 3, many people with chronic migraines find that their migraines are triggered by stress, extreme light or noise, and the weather—especially rainy or snowy conditions or hot and humid weather. Some migraineurs identify food triggers, such as alcohol, foods that include monosodium glutamate (MSG), or aspartame. Excessive caffeine consumption may also trigger a migraine.

In some cases, other medications that patients may take can make them more susceptible to developing chronic migraines. This is particularly true in the case of drugs that contain hormones, such as oral contraceptives or hormone replacement therapy medications.

Other Causes

Some experts believe that patients with chronic migraines have very sensitive nervous systems that are acutely vulnerable to either internal or external stimuli. (An example of internal stimuli would be severe stress.) Simply put, their threshold to have a headache is set at a lower level than others. With stressors (triggers), they exceed their threshold and have migraines. Thus, if they encounter certain headache triggers, this sensitivity will escalate, causing a migraine. This may be particularly true in the case of patients who have migraine with aura.

Some causes of migraines are unusual, and that's why they're difficult to diagnose. Rarely, migraines may be caused by exposure to carbon monoxide. In one report in a 1997 issue of *Headache*, a 58-year-old woman had suffered from migraines for years; but only when she went to her vacation home in Connecticut. An investigation finally revealed that she had a defective furnace that was leaking carbon monoxide. It was sufficient to cause headaches, but not extreme enough to kill her. Her migraines had been controlled with Imitrex, but once the furnace was fixed, she no longer needed the drug.

Other Coexisting Medical Problems Are Common

Some people who suffer from chronic migraines also have other medical problems, such as depression or epilepsy. When patients have two or more medical problems, doctors call them *comorbidities*. This has nothing to do with death or dying, and simply means that the person has more than one serious medical problem. These problems may have some relationship to each other, but they also may not.

If the migraine patient has a comorbid condition such as depression or epilepsy, some medications will help treat both conditions. For example, antidepressants may resolve depression and also provide pain relief to people with chronic migraines. Anti-seizure medications (particularly Topamax) may provide relief from both seizures and headache pain, although you need not have epilepsy in order to benefit from the preventive possibilities of Topamax.

Menstrual Migraines

It doesn't seem fair, but hormones can really play a number on the heads of some women. As many as 60 percent of women with migraines suffer from extreme migraine pain either during or just before their periods. Some experts have linked a deficiency of magnesium to this problem. The magnesium blood levels of women generally drop down before the onset of menstruation; and if they should drop too low, this may trigger a migraine in some women. Levels of estrogen also drop at the same time, which may be the cause of the menstrual migraine (also known as the catamenial migraine).

In one study of women with menstrual migraines, reported in *Neurology* in 2000, the researchers studied 81 menstruating women who had been previously diagnosed with migraines. They found that the greatest risk of developing a migraine was on the first and second day of menstruation. Some women, particularly women who had migraine without aura, developed migraines two days before their periods occurred.

Some women with menstrual migraines improve greatly during pregnancy, especially during the second and third trimester, when their estrogen levels are high.

Treating Menstrual Migraines

Medications are usually needed to treat the menstrual migraine, and triptans are effective for many patients. In one study reported in *Neurology* in 2004, researchers studied 546 female subjects. They were either in the placebo group (which received no drugs), the group that received Frova (frovatriptan) daily, or in another group in which the subjects were given Frova twice a day.

The researchers found that Frova reduced the incidence of menstrual migraines. The placebo group had a headache incidence of 67 percent. The group that was given the drug once daily had an incidence of 52 percent. The group that received the drug twice daily had a headache incidence of 41 percent. Of course, no migraines would have been preferable, but the drug clearly did give improvements for many women.

Other studies have shown that Imitrex (sumatriptan) and Max-alt (rizatriptan), both triptan medications, have been effective in treating menstrual migraines.

In some cases, women who suffer from menstrual migraines and take oral contraceptives, with the usual one week off the drug, are advised to take their oral contraceptives every day, with no breaks, to avoid the menstrual migraine. Your physician can advise your gynecologist about the feasibility of this course of action for you.

Women who suffer from frequent menstrual migraines may benefit from taking preventive medications, such as ergotamine, beta blockers, calcium channel blockers, or antidepressants (discussed more in Chapter 10). In addition, some women benefit from sublingual doses of estradiol. If you take estradiol during the aura phase of a menstrual migraine you may be able to head off the headache altogether.

Other Hormonal Headaches

Menstruation is not the only cause of the hormonal headache, although it's the number one cause. Other hormonal causes of migraines include birth control pills as well as the use of hormone replacement therapy (HRT) taken by menopausal women. If you take birth control pills or HRT and you also suffer from severe headaches, your doctor may be able to change your dosage or switch you to another medication.

Finding Migraine Relief—Yes, It's Out There!

Most people with chronic severe migraines need a three-step approach to managing their headaches. They need:

- A plan to address acute headaches that occur as well as a preventive plan to help limit the number of migraines as well as their severity; of course, zero migraines would be really nice, but even the best physicians can't promise to cure you of all your chronic migraines
- A plan to identify and cope with your headache triggers and gain greater control
- A plan to alleviate as much stress as possible from your life, because stress is a migraine trigger for the majority of people who suffer from them

Take Your Medicine

You need a plan to cope with a migraine when it hits. This usually involves taking medication, such as medication for an acute attack, usually a triptan medication. And don't wait to take your medicine, thinking that maybe the headache will go away if you wish it away. It won't! Take the medicine as soon as your headache symptoms start. Read about migraine-specific medications such as triptans, other headache medications, and antinausea drugs (antiemetics) that are often used to stop nausea and vomiting, in Chapter 10.

In addition to treating as many migraines as possible, preventive medications are also important. If you suffer from two or more headaches per month, or if your one headache per month causes significant disability, then preventive treatment is for you. Many physicians prescribe a variety of different types of medications to prevent chronic migraines, including beta blockers, calcium channel blockers, antidepressants, and anti-seizure medications. Supplements such as magnesium, riboflavin, and melatonin (discussed in Chapter 11) are sometimes used; and Botox therapy (covered in Chapter 12) may also provide relief for some patients suffering from chronic migraines.

Identify Your Triggers and Avoid Them When Possible

When you determine what your headache triggers are by taking our self-evaluation in Chapter 3, you can plan to avoid these substances or situations whenever possible. No matter how much you love chocolate or caffeinated drinks, if they induce a migraine, then stay away from them!

Some triggers can't be avoided, such as weather changes. But even with weather changes that cause migraines, you can plan ahead, be aware of weather reports, and take preemptive action if you feel a headache coming on. Or, if perfume sets you off, let others know you're sensitive to perfume and that it gives you migraines. Some migraineurs tell others that they are allergic to perfume. This isn't technically true, because their bodies don't create histamines in response to the perfume. But people may respond better to hearing about a severe allergy rather than being told that perfume causes a headache. Many people have no idea how painful a migraine is, and they equate the word "headache" with a minor temporary problem. But if these same people think you have an allergy, they may be more considerate to you.

Limit Stress

Everyone who's alive has to face some periods of stress, whether it's from a tough job, a difficult teenager they're coping with, or maybe both problems. You can't eliminate all stress from your life, but you can work to limit its effect on you. Since stress is a major migraine trigger for most people, it's important to develop strategies to control it.

Here are some basic do's and don'ts to help you limit your stress:

- Get at least seven hours of sleep each night.
- Don't skip meals.
- Consider learning relaxation therapy or another stress-reducing technique. (We offer suggestions for these in Chapter 13.)
- Recognize your own personal signs of stress, whether it's your neck muscles tensing, your stomach tightening up, or other signals that your body is stressing out. (It's easier to take action when you know you're starting to get stressed than after you're maximally stressed out. Also, migraine medication works better when you take it early on in the headache stage rather than later, when it has to work much harder.)
- If you fear that stress is probably going to lead to a headache, consider taking one of your preventive medications, such as Topamax.
- Try to limit stressful events that you may have lined up until your migraines are under better control. Be kind to yourself! Your body will thank you with fewer headaches.

In addition to migraine headaches and cervicogenic headaches, there are other major types of severe chronic headaches, such as cluster headaches, tension-type headaches, rebound headaches (headaches caused by your pain medication), chronic daily headaches, and combination headaches. We cover all of these different headache types in the next chapter.

CHAPTER 8

Cluster, Tension-Type, Emergency, and Other Chronic Severe Headaches

You may not have migraines or cervicogenic headaches, but you're still in agony from your chronic head pain. Maybe you're losing sleep and have trouble working or really doing much of anything when you have these severe headaches. It's a real problem; and don't let anyone tell you that if it's not a migraine or a cervicogenic headache, then you have nothing to worry about. In some cases, you could have a serious health problem, while in others, it could be a chronic nonemergency headache problem that you and your doctor first need to identify and then manage.

For example, you may be suffering from chronic cluster headaches, tension-type headaches, or occipital neuralgia. In some cases, an extremely severe headache, unlike one you've ever experienced before, should serve as an alarm to you because it's an emergency headache—possibly indicating an impending stroke, hemorrhage, or infection. Some people have painful combination headaches, with elements of two or more headache types, which can be difficult to diagnose and treat. There are also some patients (and we hope you're not one of them!) who have headaches nearly every day, with no time off from their pain.

Coping with Cluster Headaches

Cluster headaches are very painful one-sided (unilateral) headaches that generally last from 15 to 90 minutes; and then they're gone until the next one—which may occur within a few hours, days, or weeks, depending on the patient. Then the headaches may disappear altogether for a time, only to reappear again later on, for no apparent reason. Because these headaches frequently appear together over a fairly short term (such as days or weeks), they are said to "cluster," or bunch up, over a varying time interval.

Just because they don't last that long doesn't mean that cluster headaches are easily tolerated. They are actually worse than migraines in terms of their sheer excruciating pain. They also generate a reaction different from that of migraine patients. In contrast to the patient with a migraine who wants to remain as still and quiet as possible, the patient with cluster headache often feels compelled to thrash about frantically. (Not that moving around helps any. It doesn't.)

Symptoms of Cluster Headaches

In addition to severe head pain, cluster headaches are often accompanied by such symptoms as watery eyes and runny nose. Because of these symptoms, individuals with chronic cluster headaches are sometimes misdiagnosed with allergies, a sinus headache, a migraine, or even dental problems.

Patients may wake up from a deep sleep with a painful cluster headache. In fact, individuals who are prone to cluster headaches are more likely to have nighttime headaches than other headache sufferers, possibly because of a problem with their sleep-wake cycle. Sometimes melatonin supplements (discussed in Chapter 11) can improve this condition.

Patients may also experience sweating in the face and forehead. Their eyes may show symptoms of cluster headache; for example, *eyelid edema* (eyelids that are enlarged because they are full of water) is one symptom of a cluster headache. Another symptom of the eyes is *ptosis*, which is a temporarily droopy eyelid. Some patients may also experience sensitivity to light (photophobia) and sound (phonophobia), which are both symptoms that may cause doctors to misdiagnose migraine in a patient with cluster headaches. However, in contrast to many patients with migraines, those with cluster headaches usually don't experience nausea and vomiting.

Cluster Headaches Are Seen More Frequently in Men

According to the National Headache Foundation in Chicago, Illinois, there are about a million people in the United States who suffer from cluster headaches and about 20 percent of them have a chronic problem.

Men between the ages of 20 and 50 years old are the primary sufferers of cluster headaches. In fact, men develop about 90 percent of all cluster headaches, although no one knows why this is true. This doesn't mean that women can't get cluster headaches—they can and do suffer from them, although it's much less of a prevalent problem among females.

Causes and Triggers of Cluster Headaches

Genetics may play a role in cluster headaches. Some studies have indicated that first-degree relatives (children or siblings) of patients who have cluster headaches are between 5 to 18 times more likely than others to suffer from cluster headaches. To date, no gene for cluster headache has been identified.

There are also a few triggers that are specific to people who suffer from chronic cluster headaches. Alcohol is a frequent trigger of cluster headaches; and smoking can also cause cluster headaches in some individuals, as can secondhand smoke. Some studies have shown that cluster headaches seem to be a seasonal problem, occurring more often in the spring or fall, which is why they may be misdiagnosed as allergy headaches (discussed in Chapter 9).

In addition to a possible genetic link and triggers associated with cluster headaches, some research also indicates that these headaches appear to be linked to an abnormality in the hypothalamus of the brain, which is the part of the brain that controls the sleep-wake cycles. This may be why cluster headache sufferers often develop a headache in their sleep. Cluster headaches are also linked to inflammation in the trigeminal nerve in the cheek and the blood vessels in the brain.

Medications and Treatments That May Help

The problem with treating cluster headaches is that although they are severe, they are often here and then gone again before any medication that you take by mouth can have a chance to kick in and provide you with some significant relief. In the case of an acute cluster headache, doctors may administer nasal oxygen through a nasal cannula, and this treatment is very effective. The trouble usually lies in seeing the doctor right away so that you could receive this treatment in time, whether it's your regular doctor or even an emergency room physician.

Medications such as Imitrex (sumatriptan) that are injected subcutaneously (just under the skin) may provide significant pain relief to the cluster headache sufferer. (Imitrex may also be given intranasally.) In addition, prescription lidocaine nose drops administered inside the nose may sometimes stop a painful cluster headache in its tracks.

When patients suffer from chronic cluster headaches, doctors also look for preventive measures. Medications (discussed more in Chapter 10) such as calcium channel blocker medications, as well as prednisone or other steroids, or even lithium, may be given. Topamax (topiramate), an anti-seizure drug that is effective in treating other chronic headaches such as migraines, has been shown to help patients with chronic cluster headaches as well.

More recently, botulinum toxin A, or Botox (covered in Chapter 12), has proved helpful in some cases. As mentioned, even something as simple as oxygen can help certain headaches.

Tension-Type Headaches

Tension-type headaches are very common and nearly everyone in the population has had at least one tension headache in their lifetime. These headaches don't really become problematic unless they become severe and chronic in your life. These headaches can also be misdiagnosed, and many individuals who've been diagnosed with tension-type headaches actually have cervicogenic headaches.

According to the World Health Organization, 80 percent of females and 67 percent of males in developed countries have experienced tension headaches. Many people take Tylenol (acetaminophen) or aspirin for this headache, and they feel better in an hour or so. However, some sufferers, especially people with chronic tension-type headaches, need other medications and therapies.

Causes of Tension-Type Headaches

Experts disagree on the mechanism by which most people develop tension-type headaches. Some experts believe it is primarily caused by muscle contractions in the neck. Others think that both the tension headache and the migraine are on the same headache continuum, with migraine being a worse headache.

Many experts believe that tension headaches may be caused by a variety of factors, such as stress, external triggers, or even headache medications themselves. When frequent use of headache medications (over-the-counter or prescribed) leads to the development of headaches, this is called a rebound headache (discussed in Chapter 9).

Tension-Type Headache Triggers

Stress is the most frequent trigger for the tension headache, accounting for up to 80 percent of all tension-type headaches.

Another common trigger is changes in an individual's sleep schedule (either not enough sleep or oversleeping). A missed meal can trigger a tension headache in some patients, while excessive physical activity will lead to this type of headache in others. There are also some foods that are linked to the development of tension headaches, particularly alcohol, chocolate, cheese, and items that contain caffeine.

Medications can lead to tension headaches, and sometimes these are the same medications that are used to treat headaches, such as painkillers, butalbital combinations, ergot, and narcotic painkillers. In this case, a rebound headache has developed.

Other medications can also cause tension headaches, such as medications for high blood pressure, antidepressants in the selective serotonin reuptake inhibitor class (such as Prozac), and nitrates given to treat heart patients.

Symptoms in Chronic Tension-Type Headaches

Patients with chronic tension-type headaches say that the headache is like a vise-like pain around their heads. The pain is often present on both sides of the head (bilateral) in contrast to other headaches types such as migraines, which usually hurt on only one side of the head. The pain of the tension headache may last for under an hour or up to a week; and the headache duration varies greatly from patient to patient. Many tension headache patients say that they feel tired, irritable, and distracted.

Treatment for Tension-Type Headaches

Simple over-the-counter painkillers usually won't resolve chronic tension-type headaches, especially when they occur more than two days per week. Most patients will need prescribed medications, such as muscle relaxants like Flexeril (cyclobenzaprine) to cope with an acute attack. A low dose of a NSAID may help stem the pain; however, patients with cardiovascular risks for a heart attack or stroke should avoid NSAIDs when possible. (Talk to your doctor about whether NSAIDs could present a risk to you.)

Some patients with tension-type headaches improve with Imitrex (sumatriptan), a drug routinely used with migraines. Research has shown that those patients who gain the greatest benefit from Imitrex are also patients who complain of throbbing headaches and who are very sensitive to light and sound. They also experience greater headache pain subsequent to exercise.

During an active headache, many physicians recommend heat or ice, or prescribed muscle relaxants and/or painkillers. Other patients may find relief from alternative therapies, such as acupuncture, *transcutaneous electrical nerve stimulation (TENS)*, massage therapy, and/or biofeedback, discussed in Chapter 13. In addition, some patients with tension headaches improve with Botox therapy.

Avoidance of extreme stress is a very good idea for the person who suffers from recurrent tension-type headaches. If you can't avoid severe stress, learn and adopt good ways to cope with stress, such as relaxation therapy. Some patients may benefit from psychotherapy when their personal problems are overwhelming. If you see a therapist, it doesn't mean your headaches are imaginary. They're real. But your high stress levels may be inducing your headaches. When a therapist can help you devise better ways to cope with personal problems, your stress levels will often abate, as will your severe headaches.

Occipital Neuralgia

Some chronic-headache patients suffer from *occipital neuralgia*, a disorder that is caused by an injury or irritation to the occipital nerves that lie in the back of the scalp and extend to the second and third vertebrae in the neck. This headache causes a severe and throbbing migraine-like pain in the head. The pain may be on one side (unilateral) or both sides of the head (bilateral). It usually worsens with neck movements. Some patients may also experience dizziness, nausea, and/or tinnitus (ringing in the ears). Rarely, patients with occipital neuralgia may experience eye pain.

Both men and women suffer equally from occipital neuralgia and they may be of any age. Unlike most other headache types, occipital neuralgia is an equal-opportunity offender.

Not surprisingly, headaches caused by occipital neuralgia may often be misdiagnosed as either migraines or tension-type headaches. Diagnosis can be very tricky, and it is generally only made by an experienced physician who is knowledgeable about all types of headaches. We hate to keep plugging neurologists (well okay, we don't!), but who knows the most about the brain and spinal cord? Ring that buzzer. The answer is: neurologists.

Causes of Occipital Neuralgia

Occipital neuralgia may result from trauma to the head, such as trauma caused from a car accident. It is more specific than whiplash because a specific nerve is damaged. Sometimes athletes may develop occipital neuralgia, especially when they hyperextend their heads. Osteoarthritis and disk disease can cause occipital neuralgia. Rarely, patients with occipital neuralgia may have a tumor. However, often physicians cannot determine the cause. (Doctors can rule out the presence of a tumor with imaging tests, such as an MRI.)

Treating Occipital Neuralgia

Nerve blocks in the cervical spine are the most effective treatment for occipital neuralgia; however, health insurance companies may regard this treatment as experimental or investigational and thus, refuse to provide coverage. Physicians may also inject steroids in the painful area, which helps some patients. (A local anesthetic is given first, so you won't feel the pain when the injection is given.)

Massage therapy may provide temporary relief from occipital neuralgia, and acupuncture may also be helpful. Botox therapy may be useful, although research has not upheld Botox for the treatment of occipital neuralgia.

Prescribed medications are often needed by the patient with chronic pain from occipital neuralgia, such as muscle relaxants.

Sometimes anti-seizure drugs such as Tegretol (carbamazepine) are given. Antidepressants may be prescribed when the pain is severe and chronic.

Patients with very severe chronic pain that don't respond to medication or other therapies may receive surgery to help break the pain cycle, such as *radiofrequency thermocoagulation (RF)* or *pulsed radiofrequency (PRF)*. If patients have disk disease, surgery on the cervical spine may improve the condition. Some physicians numb or deaden part of the offending nerve with procedures such as the *partial posterior rhizotomy*, giving some patients significant pain relief.

Some patients with very painful occipital neuralgia have an electrical nerve stimulator implanted into their cervical spine. Although it sounds like a very scary procedure, most physicians actually consider it to be minor surgery. The electrical nerve stimulator will not destroy the surrounding nerves or tissue. Studies of very small numbers of patients (19 patients in one study and 13 in another) have revealed that patients with occipital neuralgia obtained major pain relief from implanted electrical nerve stimulators. This "electrical noise" seems to interfere with pain impulse transmission within the central nervous system.

Emergency Headaches

Some forms of headaches are either medical emergencies or they are warnings that something really bad is coming up, and that you need medical attention urgently and immediately. Strokes are often preceded by an extremely severe headache, as are aneurysms of the brain (burst blood clots). Based on a study of more than 35,000 Finnish men and women, reported in the *Archives of Internal Medicine* in 2003, men with chronic headaches, especially between the ages of 25 and 49, have a higher risk of stroke than women, but women are not immune from sudden strokes. The risk for stroke was higher among smokers than nonsmokers, and obese people had a greater stroke risk.

Linking Chronic Daily Headaches with Rebound Headaches and Other Causes

In a study in Spain of nearly 10,000 people, reported in *Neurology* in 2004, the researchers found 332 subjects had chronic headaches for 10 days a month and of these subjects, 74 met the criteria for chronic daily headache with analgesic overuse. Of the patients who overused painkillers, most of them overused simple analgesics (35 percent) or drug combinations (27.8 percent), followed by those who used ergots to excess (22 percent) or opiates (12.5 percent). Only 2.7 percent had overused triptan medications.

Another study reported in *Neurology* in 2004 found that subjects who overused their painkillers were more than seven times more likely to suffer from chronic daily headaches than those who did not overuse them. Clearly, the rebound headache is a serious problem for many people.

In another study, reported in *Headache* in 2002, researchers looked for correlations between chronic headaches and allergies, hypothyroidism, hypertension, and other factors. They divided the patients into one group with chronic migraines that was associated with analgesic overuse, a second group of patients with chronic migraines who did *not* overuse analgesics, and a third group of patients with a "new daily persistent headache." These three groups were then compared to two control groups—one group in which the subjects had episodic migraines and another group in

If you or someone you know is suffering from a headache that is the most severe headache you or they ever experienced, get emergency medical help. Don't wait for your regular doctor to call you back. Call 911. Don't drive yourself to the hospital emergency room because you may become sicker or could become unconscious on the way there, risking your life and the lives of others in a car crash. Instead, go there by ambulance. If you can't

which the patients suffered from chronic posttraumatic headaches (headaches that occurred either after surgery or a severe injury). The researchers found that the study groups, when compared to the control group with episodic migraines, had the following associations. The group with chronic migraines with analgesic overuse had significant associations with hypertension and daily caffeine consumption. The group with chronic migraines *without* analgesic overuse had significant links to allergies, asthma, hypothyroidism, hypertension, and the daily consumption of caffeine. Last, the group with new daily persistent headache had significant links to allergies, asthma, hypothyroidism, and alcohol consumption that occurred more than three times per week. When the three study groups were then compared to the control group of patients with chronic posttraumatic headaches, the researchers found the following associations: For patients with chronic migraines and analgesic overuse, the associations that stood out were asthma and hypertension. For patients with chronic migraines without analgesic overuse, the associations were allergies, asthma, hypothyroidism, hypertension, and daily caffeine consumption. And for patients with new daily persistent headaches, the associations were allergies, asthma, hypothyroidism, and alcohol consumption more than three times per week.

get an ambulance, ask a family member, friend, or neighbor to drive you to the hospital right away. Tell the person it's a medical emergency. Even most people you barely know would be willing to help you out in such a situation.

What if you're wrong and it turns out *not* to be a stroke or an aneurysm, but it's a migraine or another headache instead? That's good news, so be happy. But if it *is* a stroke, immediate medical attention may save your life as well as help to preserve your physical and mental functioning. The recovery from a stroke can be very difficult when treatment is delayed.

Combination/Mixed Headaches

Maybe you have *only* migraines, cluster headaches, cervicogenic headaches, or one of the other forms of headaches that we describe in this book. However, many people suffer from combination/mixed headaches, which have elements of two or more different headaches. You may also have migraines on some days and tension-type headaches on other days, but that's not the same thing as a combination headache. Instead, with a combination headache, you have both types of headaches at the *same* time. Pretty awful to contemplate, isn't it? It's worse to experience it.

Combination headaches are difficult to diagnose, so make sure your doctor is experienced and interested in treating headaches; otherwise, the doctor may miss this diagnosis altogether. You may need several different medications to treat the combination headache, and the drugs that are needed depend on the headache types that you're suffering from.

Chronic Daily Headaches

Some people suffer from headaches every—or nearly every—day. This is a truly cruel fate. The daily chronic headache is a problem for people with many types of headaches, but it's most frequent among patients who overuse their over-the-counter and prescription painkillers. In general, people with chronic daily headaches have headaches for at least 10–15 days each month.

Causes of Chronic Daily Headache

As a result of the findings in all these studies, individuals with chronic daily headaches should be tested for allergies, asthma, hypertension, and hypothyroidism (discussed in Chapter 9). If patients have one or more of these medical problems, they need treatment, such as antihistamines, asthma medication, blood pressure medication, or thyroid medications. Patients who drink caffeine each day should taper off and see if their headaches improve. In addition, alcohol consumption should be sharply curtailed, or better yet, it should cease altogether.

Medications for Chronic Daily Headaches

Most patients with chronic daily headaches need medication. Some patients are treated with antidepressants, particularly Elavil (amitriptyline) or Prozac (fluoxetine). Remeron (mirtazapine) is a newer antidepressant that has been shown effective in treating chronic tension-type headaches. In addition, patients with frequent chronic tension-type headaches may be treated with muscle relaxants, such as Skelaxin (metaxalone) or Soma (carisprodol). Topamax may also be used to prevent the development of frequent tension headaches.

Now that we have addressed other types of severe headaches, continue on to the next chapter to find out about headaches that are caused by other medical problems, such as hypothyroidism, allergies, sinus infections, and sleep disorders (for example, obstructive sleep apnea).

CHAPTER 9

When Headache Pain Stems from Other Medical Conditions or Causes

Lucy, 37, thought she had migraines and her doctor agreed, so he gave her a triptan drug specifically meant to combat migraine headaches. But the medication didn't help, and her headaches just kept coming, nearly every day. Her doctor decided to do a complete workup on Lucy, including a physical examination and laboratory work. A simple blood test revealed that Lucy was anemic and that she needed to take iron supplements. She followed her doctor's advice, and the headaches went away, along with her anemia.

Of course it isn't always this simple. But a surprising number of people with chronic headaches have other underlying medical problems that are often treatable—and that *should* be treated before the problem escalates any further. They may have metabolic diseases, such as thyroid disease or diabetes. Some people have hypertension that hasn't been diagnosed; while others have chronic infections, such as sinusitis. Others suffer from chronic allergies. Patients with many other serious illnesses, such as asthma, systemic lupus erythematosus (SLE), or multiple sclerosis, are prone to chronic headaches.

In some cases, it may be the headache medication itself that you take that is causing chronic severe headaches, and these "rebound" headaches won't go away until the problem is identified and tackled.

Your headaches may also result from a problem with your eyes, or it could be caused by a *temporomandibular disorder* (stemming from a problem with the jaw area). This chapter provides an overview of the more common medical problems that may cause chronic headaches. Please keep in mind, however, that there are numerous diagnoses that can lead to headaches, and your doctor is the best person to identify and treat your chronic headache problem.

How Doctors Suspect Your Headaches May Be Something Else

When the medications that normally help with headaches don't work at all, your doctor will usually suspect that the headaches may have a cause other than brain pain or referred pain from the neck, as with cervicogenic headaches. Of course, it's best if doctors do a complete workup with a chronic headache patient before they prescribe medications or treatments. But sometimes the diagnosis seems obvious to the doctor, and thus, he'll write a prescription for a migraine medication or another headache remedy before ordering any laboratory or imaging tests. When these medications provide little or no relief, the doctor realizes (or should realize!) that more medical detective work is in order.

Maybe the doctor has misdiagnosed your headache type, and you really have migraines instead of tension-type headaches or sinus headaches. Don't forget, you may have many different types of headaches, which is very common and often bedevils headache management. Or you may have an underlying illness that is the driving force in your headaches. Both possibilities should be considered by you and your doctor.

Common Illnesses That Cause Chronic Headaches

A variety of medical problems can induce headaches, and when these illnesses are not diagnosed or treated, the headaches will inevitably continue. This section covers the most prominent problems that can lead to frequent headaches.

Thyroid Disease Can Cause Chronic Headaches

Patients with thyroid disease, particularly low levels of circulating thyroid hormone (hypothyroidism), may experience chronic headaches. Hypothyroidism is very common and Hashimoto's thyroiditis is the most common form of hypothyroidism. Patients with hypothyroidism may be lethargic, and they may also have an enlarged neck (goiter). They are usually very sensitive to cold temperatures and their skin may appear cool and dry.

In a study of 102 patients with hypothyroidism, ages 35 to 78 years old, reported in a 1998 issue of *Cephalgia*, 30 percent of the subjects developed chronic headaches after the onset of their illness. These patients did not have severe headaches, although some patients with untreated hypothyroidism do suffer from very painful headaches. When the patients in the study were treated with thyroid hormone, their headaches went away completely.

At the other end of the thyroid spectrum, hyperthyroidism, or too much circulating thyroid hormone, can also cause chronic headaches. This may be because of the elevated blood pressure that may accompany this disorder. Patients with hyperthyroidism are sensitive to hot temperatures, and their skin is often warm and moist. Graves' disease is the most common form of hyperthyroidism; and patients with Graves' disease often present with nervousness. They may also have an enlarged neck, similar to patients with hypothyroidism. Some patients have a bulging-eye appearance. It should be noted, however, that patients older than age 65 with hyperthyroidism might appear lethargic rather than hyperactive.

Both hypothyroidism and hyperthyroidism are diagnosed with the thyroid-stimulating hormone (TSH) test, a simple blood test. If the test results are on the low side, then the person may be diagnosed with hyperthyroidism. If they are on the high side, then the patient probably has hypothyroidism. (We know that this sounds wrong, because intuitively, it seems like a low test result should indicate a low thyroid level and a high test result should indicate hyperthyroidism. But low TSH test results mean hyper-thyroidism and high TSH results mean hypothyroidism, for com-plicated reasons. Trust us on this one.)

Hypothyroidism is generally treated with levothyroxine, a pre-scribed thyroid hormone. Hyperthyroidism is tougher to treat and is often treated with Tapazole, a drug that is used to suppress the thyroid gland. The disorder may also be treated with radiation therapy. In some cases, removal of the thyroid gland (thyroidec-tomy) is indicated; and patients will subsequently take thyroid pills after their surgery, for life.

If thyroid disease is causing your frequent headaches, resolv-ing your thyroid problem should give you significant headache relief.

Diabetes and Headaches

Diabetes may induce headaches in some patients. There are two types of diabetes: Type 1 diabetes and Type 2 diabetes.

Type 1 is less common and represents about 5–10 percent of all diabetes cases. It is usually diagnosed in childhood or adoles-cence but occasionally is diagnosed in young adults. Patients with this form of diabetes need insulin to live, usually in the form of injections. Patients with Type 1 diabetes have a problem in that their pancreas cannot produce *any* insulin, yet insulin is needed to stay alive. Before the discovery of insulin in 1921 by Dr. Banting, a Canadian physician, and Dr. Best, a Canadian medical student at the time, everyone who had Type 1 diabetes died. Now with regular blood testing (at least twice a day), monitoring of the diet, and regular medical checkups, most people with Type 1 diabetes can lead normal lives.

Type 2 diabetes is more common, and it often isn't diagnosed until adulthood. People with Type 2 diabetes are likely to be over-weight or obese. They usually don't need insulin unless their ill-ness becomes severe; and instead they rely upon oral medications to help them normalize their blood sugar levels. In the case of people with Type 2 diabetes, their bodies usually create some insulin, but they have an insulin resistance—which means that their bodies can't use all the insulin that is made. As a result, they require medication to maintain normal blood sugar levels.

Without treatment, patients with diabetes are generally hyper-glycemic, which means they have too much glucose (blood sugar) in their blood. However, they can easily swing to hypoglycemia, which refers to inadequate blood sugar levels; and this condition causes severe headaches and can lead to serious complications or even death. Don't assume that diabetics should never eat foods with sugar. Sometimes they urgently need such foods, depending on their blood sugar levels.

High or Low Blood Pressure Leads to Headaches in Many People

Most doctors readily diagnose *hypertension* (high blood pressure) by the measurements that the nurse or doctor takes with a blood pressure cuff. However, maybe you haven't seen the doctor for a long time or hypertension is a new problem for you. One symp-tom of hypertension is severe headaches. If your headaches stem from hypertension, stabilizing your blood pressure should decrease the frequency and intensity of your headaches. Of course, it's also important to treat hypertension for many other reasons. Untreated hypertension can lead to a stroke or heart attack.

It's also true that unusually low blood pressure (*hypotension*) can cause headaches. Hypotension is sometimes induced by medications, although there are many other causes. Your physician can help you determine the cause and the solution.

Anemia and Headaches

Many people suffer from a low level of anemia, as did Lucy at the beginning of this chapter. The anemia may be related to other illnesses they have or to iron or vitamin B_{12} deficiencies. Hospitalized patients who are ill with serious medical problems are at risk for anemia, which is one reason why their blood is frequently tested during their hospital stay. Whatever the cause of anemia, one symptom is the severe headache. However, when your doctor discovers that you have anemia and treats it, the headaches should disappear or at least decrease in intensity.

Allergy Headaches

Every spring, Sharon suffered from near-daily headaches. Her garden was in bloom, the trees were all flowering, but Sharon was miserable. Her nose was running, her eyes were streaming, and her headaches were awful. Her headaches stemmed from very bad allergies to pollen, as she later discovered.

For Aleisha, it wasn't the season that mattered. She had headaches all year round. After undergoing skin and blood tests for allergies, Aleisha discovered that she was severely allergic to her cat Bubbles. Aleisha began receiving allergy shots (because she couldn't bear to give up Bubbles), and the headaches abated.

Both Sharon and Aleisha, along with millions of other people in the United States and Canada, suffer from chronic allergies. Headache is a common symptom of allergy, although other symptoms are present as well, such as rhinitis (nose inflammation) and tearing eyes.

Patients with headaches associated with inflammatory nasal disease can be treated with antihistamines, nasal corticosteroids, and decongestants. Prevention is also important; avoiding headache triggers reduces the risk of getting a headache. In some cases, patients can use prescribed lidocaine sprays to decrease their headache symptoms.

Linking Headaches with Allergies

In one study of patients with rhinologic headaches (headaches associated with a nasal condition), reported in a 2004 issue of *Allergy and Asthma Proceedings*, the researchers studied 66 patients whose primary complaint was headache, and who also had nasal problems such as enlargements, septal spurs, septal deviation, polyps, and other problems excluding sinusitis. These patients said their headache lasted for hours and occurred around the eyes.

Among these patients, 68 percent positively reacted to at least one of the 33 allergens they were tested on, and most positively reacted to more than one allergen. (An allergen is a substance that induces an allergic response.) The largest percentages among those who were allergic tested positive to an allergy for dust mites (48 percent), trees (35 percent), weeds (33 percent), and cats (33 percent). (These percentages don't add up to 100 percent since many patients were allergic to more than one allergen.)

The researchers also found common headache triggers for the subjects. (As with allergens, many patients reacted to more than one trigger.) The most common headache trigger was cigarette smoke (67 percent), followed by strong odors (62 percent), humidity (60 percent), dust (58 percent), cold air (55 percent), mold (49 percent), and perfume (46 percent). According to the researchers, rhinitis patients who also suffer from headaches need treatment for both problems; and "properly diagnosed nasal disease may result in significant headache improvement, along with relief from other symptoms more commonly associated with rhinitis."

Asthma

Some studies indicate that people with asthma are at greater risk for headaches than others. Asthma is a chronic respiratory disease that causes inflammation of the airways and leads to severe coughing and shortness of breath. In some cases it is the extreme coughing that may cause headaches. If not treated, an asthmatic person can die. About 10 million adults and 5 million children in the United States suffer from asthma.

Experts believe that asthma is primarily an allergic disease, and common triggers are dust mites, household pets, and perfumes. It is also a hereditary disease, and according to the Centers for Disease Control and Prevention (CDC), the child of a parent with asthma is three to six times more likely to develop the illness than children whose parents are asthma-free.

Asthma is treated with quick-relief medications in an emergency—such as short-acting bronchodilators that help open up airways fast so the patient can breathe. Patients with asthma also need long-term treatment—usually in the form of inhaled corticosteroids and antihistamines. When asthma is under good control, headache problems should also improve.

Sinus Headaches/Sinusitis

Many people think sinus headaches are the same as allergy headaches and in fact, they are very similar. However, sinusitis is caused by a bacterial infection in the sinus passages rather than by the internal release of substances known as histamines in response to an allergy to flowers, cats, or something else. Sinusitis is usually preceded by the common cold. The person's resistance is down and bacteria move in and take over.

The sinus headache can be extremely painful. It may respond to allergy medications, but if your problem is sinusitis, you need to take antibiotics too.

Sinusitis in adults can last from one to three months if it isn't treated; and the longer the condition remains untreated, the more likely it is to become a chronic problem that is difficult to treat. However, it's important to note, as we discussed in the migraine chapter, that many patients with migraines are misdiagnosed with sinusitis, primarily because the migrainous patients had a runny nose and tearing eyes.

Symptoms of Sinusitis

The common symptoms of a sinus infection are facial pain, pressure, and congestion; as well as nasal problems, such as a blockage or heavy mucus discharge. The sense of smell is often impaired. Patients with acute sinusitis are also feverish. Headache is considered a secondary symptom to these other symptoms; as are bad breath, tiredness, cough, and ear pain and pressure.

Doctors can diagnose sinusitis with X-rays of the head. Dentists also may be able to diagnose sinusitis, because the infected sinuses may show up on dental X-rays. However, often X-rays are not taken and patients are diagnosed based on other factors, such as headache, a runny nose, and tearing eyes. In addition, if the doctor treats a patient with migraine with antibiotics, the patient may recover from the migraine naturally within a few days, and the doctor may mistakenly attribute the improvement to the antibiotics. As a result, people who are symptomatic and may have sinusitis should also be x-rayed to confirm the diagnosis.

A nasal endoscopy can also determine the presence of sinusitis, but most patients are treated by primary care doctors who don't have access to this tool. For that procedure, you would need to go to an otolaryngologist (ear, nose, and throat doctor). If your internist has a specialty in allergy and asthma, that can also be helpful.

The good news about sinusitis is that it's treatable; and your headaches should go away once the antibiotics kick in. The bad news is that some people are prone to developing repeated sinus headaches.

Rebound Headaches

It seems so unfair but one form of headache is actually caused by the medication that you take to *treat* your headaches. The rebound headache is a medication-induced headache that is often related to taking daily doses of over-the-counter medications such as aspirin or Tylenol, or prescribed medications like Cafergot (ergotamine),

A Study to Test Treatment for Rebound Headaches

In a study reported in *Headache* in 2001, the researcher recruited 39 patients with daily or near-daily headaches who were likely to be suffering from rebound headaches. The patients were removed completely from their headache medication and over-the-counter painkillers, and if a severe headache occurred, they gave themselves an injection of dihydroergotamine mesylate. Patients were also told that if they had to go to the hospital emergency room for a headache, they should ask the ER staff for intravenous Stemetil (prochlorperazine) or Inapsine (droperidol), rather than analgesics. (ERs commonly give acute headache patients either opioids or other painkillers, and they should be avoided if possible when you're working on recovering from rebound headaches.)

Seventy-four percent (29 patients) were able to achieve six or more consecutive days without headaches, which was a treatment success. The time it took to achieve this goal varied greatly, ranging from 3 days to 325 days (with an average of 84 days). Nine of the ten remaining patients reported improvement, although they hadn't yet achieved six or more headache-free days. Only one patient was a treatment failure.

Fiornal or Fioricet (butalbital with aspirin or acetaminophen), which are covered in Chapter 10. In some cases, triptan drugs for migraines can cause rebound headaches.

Rebound headaches usually have an insidious onset. You have a severe headache or maybe another pain problem, so you take Tylenol or aspirin. Or maybe your doctor gives you a headache medication such as Cafergot or Fioricet. Maybe you feel better; but it still hurts, so you take more of the medicine. After a while, you need the medicine because your brain gets itself into a headache state without it. You're not an addict in the same way that a person taking heroin or cocaine is addicted to the drug. But there is a certain level of dependency because when you have rebound headaches, your headache will be very severe if you stop taking the drug for more than a day or so. However, rebound headaches are treatable.

Resolving the Rebound Headache

To get rid of rebound headaches, you need to break the cycle. Your doctor may advise you to taper off your usual headache remedies, or he may tell you to stop taking the medicine altogether. Some physicians give another medication to patients who are going off the medications causing their rebound headaches. They may give them subcutaneous injections of dihydroergotamine mesylate (which patients can learn to give themselves) if an extremely severe headache occurs. They may also offer a low dose of Elavil (amitriptyline), which is a mild antidepressant that is often used as an additional treatment for chronic pain. Others substitute another drug, such as phenobarbital, to provide short-term relief until the headache cycle is broken.

Don't try to alleviate your rebound headaches on your own. Enlist the help of your doctor, who may have many good suggestions to help you. And don't be afraid to tell your doctor that you wonder if you may have rebound headaches. He won't look down on you because he'll know that this is a common problem that can happen to anyone.

When Other Medications Induce Headaches

The rebound headache is caused by headache medications. But other medications can also cause headaches. If you read the list of side effects of almost any medication, headache is a common problem, no matter what the drug. In many cases, the headache goes away in a day or two as your body accustoms itself to the drug. In other cases, the headache is so severe that it's wise to consult with your doctor about whether you should decrease the medication dosage or discontinue the drug altogether.

Chronic Infections

Remember the headache, fever, and overall pain that you get when you have a bad case of the flu? A virus or bacterial infection can cause severe headaches. This is especially true if it's a chronic problem that hasn't been treated. Your body may have dealt with it sufficiently so that you aren't feverish, but the infection is still there and causing you problems.

We can't go into a lot of details on infections here because there are so many different types that people contract. However, if you seem to be always recovering from an infection or developing a new one, see your doctor to discuss tactics for regaining your health. You may need to go on a low dose of antibiotics or your doctor may recommend vitamins or other therapies.

Obstructive Sleep Apnea

Patients with *obstructive sleep apnea (OSA)*, a condition that causes sleeping patients to stop breathing for brief periods, may also cause chronic headaches. If you've been diagnosed with OSA and you have recurrent headaches, it might be wise to consider treatment. If you know that you snore frequently and loudly (because your partner or family members tell you about it or you wake yourself up), then you should be evaluated for OSA.

Temporomandibular Disorders

Teeth clenching, grinding the teeth at night, and a misalignment of the jaw are just a few oral/dental causes of headache pain. These are all symptoms of *temporomandibular disorders (TMDs)*, which are conditions that include problems with both the muscles and the joint at the jaw. Other common symptoms are facial pain, jaw pain, and clicking noises when you open and close your mouth widely. About 13 million Americans have some form of a

Investigating the Link Between Headaches and Obstructive Sleep Apnea

In one study of 80 patients with OSA, reported in a 1999 issue of *Archives of Internal Medicine*, the headache history of the patients was reviewed, and researchers found that 60 percent of the patients suffered from headaches. About half of the headaches didn't fit other headache categories, and most patients in that half (23 out of 25 patients) said the headaches occurred when they woke up in the morning. These morning headaches lasted 30 minutes or less and their severity was directly related to the severity of their OSA.

Twenty-nine of the patients were treated for their OSA with either continuous positive airway pressure or a surgical procedure—called uvulopalatopharyngoplasty. This is a long and fancy name for a surgery that removes the uvula in the throat in order to resolve sleep apnea.

About 80 percent of the patients who had awakening headaches improved with treatment, but there was very little improvement among the patients who had migraines, tension-type headaches, or cervicogenic headaches. Interestingly, patients with cluster headaches also improved with treatment of their sleep apnea.

Other researchers have not found a relationship between sleep apnea and headaches, and further research is needed.

TMD, according to James Fricton in his 2004 article on temporomandibular muscle and joint disorders in *Pain: Clinical Updates*. If headaches can't be explained by other causes, the underlying problem may be TMD.

Both men and women may suffer from TMD, but women are more likely to seek treatment than men. The problem may lie with the *temporomandibular joint* (*TMJ*), which is the joint that connects the jaw to the head—right in front of your ear. Other problems of TMD, such as teeth clenching and grinding, may be caused by stress. TMDs may also be caused by arthritis, fractures, traumatic injuries, and other causes that can be diagnosed with an MRI.

The goal of treatment is usually to alleviate pain, as well as to return the jaw to normal functioning, when possible. And if you have TMD and resolve your problem, associated headaches will also improve or go away.

Medications such as corticosteroids, muscle relaxants, opioids, antidepressants, and NSAIDs are often prescribed for TMD patients. Physical therapy may also help patients to improve jaw function, as may cryotherapy (extreme cold), ultrasound, low-intensity lasers, and massage therapy. Also equally important: don't chew gum if you have any form of TMD.

Nighttime mouth guards may resolve the problem; or if it is severe, special mouth splints are sometimes used—which are specially made for the individual patient. Other therapies are also used, such as behavior modification to train patients to avoid tensing their jaw and grinding their teeth. Experts report that even when teeth grinding occurs when the patient is asleep, if it is corrected during the day, this correction will carry over through the night.

Relaxation therapy and biofeedback are also used to treat patients with TMDs. Patients are also advised to avoid caffeine, which may increase jaw tension. Since caffeine is a major contributor to headaches anyway, this is yet another reason to cut way back or give up your coffee or soft drinks altogether.

You should also avoid leaning your jaw into your hand, as with Rodin's famous statue *The Thinker*. Think with your hands placed elsewhere and avoid straining the jaw. Don't sleep on your stomach because that puts too much pressure on your neck and jaw.

Sometimes surgery is needed by TMD patients, but make sure to try these tips and other helpful hints from your doctor or dentist before signing up for TMD surgery.

Eye Problems That May Cause Headaches

If you suffer from chronic headaches and it's been a year or more since you had your last eye examination, make an appointment for an eye checkup with an optometrist or an ophthalmologist. Your headaches may be caused by an eye problem that you didn't know about.

Chronic eye strain and/or squinting to see what's going on in the world can lead to headaches, although this is probably less common than your grandmother would have you believe. You may need glasses, or if you already wear glasses, you may need your prescription changed. Optometrists also check for eye diseases, such as glaucoma and cataracts. In addition, if your eyes are bloodshot or very dry, the optometrist should offer you some suggestions to resolve the problem.

Now that you have read about some of the many different kinds of conditions and causes of headaches, it's time to look at the next chapter, which talks about medications that may give you dramatic pain relief.

Getting to Wellness: Working with Your Doctor to Treat Your Headaches

This last section is on wellness and working with your doctor to get better. We cover the most commonly prescribed headache medications and offer a helpful chart on medications and the headache types they treat most effectively. Interested in over-the-counter medications, vitamins, or supplements? We explore that topic and discuss magnesium, riboflavin, and melatonin as possible preventive remedies, in addition to old standbys, such as Tylenol (acetaminophen). We also talk about Botox, a surprisingly effective pain therapy for many people with migraines and other headaches. It's not just for wrinkles anymore! Finally, we offer helpful advice on alternative methods that are used to treat chronic headaches—from electrical stimulation and biofeedback, to relaxation therapy, massage therapy, and other therapies—and offer practical advice on changes that you can make to lessen the frequency and severity of your headaches.

CHAPTER 10

Prescribing Relief: Medications That Combat and Prevent Recurring Headaches

Once you've worked with your doctor to identify the type of headache you have—whether it's migraines, cervicogenic headaches, or another type of headache—you'll usually need to take prescribed medications, at least some of the time. Some medications work well for most types of headaches while others are more specific to a particular type. For example, drugs in the "triptan" class are most effective at treating acute migraines, while an anticonvulsant drug known as Topamax (topiramate) is effective at preventing migraines, cluster headaches, and cervicogenic headaches. Ergot derivatives are often prescribed to treat migraines. Barbiturates, such as butalbital, are prescribed for patients with tension-type headaches and migraines. Some drugs are prescribed for symptoms other than headache. For example, antiemetic drugs are medications to help stop the nausea and vomiting that many patients with migraines suffer from.

If the pain is very severe, some people are prescribed narcotic medications, such as Percocet (oxycodone with acetaminophen) or Vicodin (hydrocodone with acetaminophen). In addition, people with chronic headaches often take other controlled drugs, such as butalbital (Fioricet, Fiornal), and sometimes they develop a dependency on the drug and/or develop rebound headaches. In most cases, headache patients should avoid narcotics because they won't resolve their headache pain and will only make them feel "druggy" and spaced out. There is a high risk of addiction to these types of medications if they're taken incorrectly. It is much better to seek help to obtain the appropriate treatment for *your* individual headache.

Never use either old narcotics from your medicine cabinet or medications from other family members, friends, or others who may offer them to you to relieve your pain.

In this chapter, we discuss the most commonly prescribed headache medications today. We also discuss medications to prevent headaches, which include drugs from specific classes of medications, including antidepressants, anti-seizure medications, beta blockers, calcium channel blockers, and topical anesthetics. At the end of the chapter, you'll find a quick reference table (Table 10.1) for the groups of medications, their brand and generic names, and the type(s) of headaches they are most effective in treating and/or preventing.

Nonsteroidal Anti-Inflammatory Drugs and COX-2 Inhibitors

Many people with chronic headaches are prescribed a NSAID to alleviate at least some of the pain. NSAIDs may be helpful in patients with tension-type headaches or cervicogenic headaches. NSAIDs block two enzymes that cause pain, cyclooxygenase-1 and cyclooxygenase-2. Some examples of commonly prescribed NSAIDs are Orudis (ketoprofen), Mobic (meloxicam), Feldene (piroxicam), Clinoril (sulindac), Relafen (nabumetone), Anaprox or Naprosyn (naproxen sodium), and Tolectin (tolmetin sodium).

Important FDA Changes Regarding COX-2 Inhibitors and NSAIDS

There has been a lot of confusing and conflicting information in the news on cyclooxygenase-2 inhibitor medications (COX-2 inhibitors)—painkilling medications that block the cyclooxygenase-2 enzyme involved with pain and inflammation. Previously, COX-2 inhibitors had become such a popular choice in managing pain because other nonsteroidal inflammatory medications (NSAIDs) that block both cycloxygenase-1 and 2 enzymes had been shown to cause stomach upset and an increased risk for ulcers and gastrointestinal bleeding. However, recently some studies have shown that patients at risk for cardiovascular disease, including heart attack and stroke, may suffer an increased risk with the chronic use of some COX-2 inhibitor medications as well as some NSAIDs.

In 2004, Merck & Co. Inc., voluntarily withdrew Vioxx (rofecoxib), a COX-2 inhibitor, from the market because of its potential cardiovascular risks and in 2005, the Food and Drug Administration (FDA) asked Pfizer, Inc., to withdraw Bextra (valdecoxib), also a COX-2 inhibitor, from the market because of its cardiovascular risks.

As of this writing, the sole remaining COX-2 inhibitor available is Celebrex (celecoxib)—also sold by Pfizer, Inc. However, the FDA has asked Pfizer to include a boxed warning on Celebrex labels to describe its potential risks, and for the inclusion of a medication guide to be given to patients to educate them about the potential risk of cardiovascular illness as well as the risk for gastrointestinal events. The FDA also asked the manufacturers of *all* prescribed NSAID drugs to revise their labels and include a boxed warning about cardiovascular and gastrointestinal risks.

We think it's important for you to realize that every medication, whether an OTC or prescribed drug, has possible side effects. In fact, although aspirin has been an OTC drug since 1905, it can cause severe gastrointestinal bleeding after prolonged use in some patients. It can also severely affect your body's ability to stop bleeding, also known as clotting. In addition, if Tylenol (acetaminophen) is taken frequently, patients risk liver disease. If aspirin or acetaminophen were introduced as new drugs now, we strongly suspect that the Food and Drug Administration (FDA) would not approve either of them as over-the-counter drugs.

Looking at Benefits and Side Effects of Prescribed NSAIDs

The primary benefit of a NSAID is that it can provide considerable pain relief and thus may be helpful for people with many different types of headaches, but particularly for those patients with tension-type headaches and cervicogenic headaches. The primary disadvantages to NSAIDs lie in their side effects, particularly gastrointestinal upset, gastrointestinal bleeding, and the fact that they cause gastric ulcers. Stress makes anyone with an ulcer or a developing ulcer feel much worse, but it doesn't directly cause them.

Who Should Not Take NSAIDs

People with any risk factors for cardiovascular disease should avoid NSAIDs, and they should also only be used with care in most patients over the age of 65. (The risk of heart attack and stroke increases with age.) In addition, patients with a past history of gastric ulcer or who are currently experiencing gastrointestinal pain when they take NSAIDs, should reconsider using an NSAID because they may cause a recurrence of the ulcer.

Ergot Derivatives

Doctors have been using ergot derivatives to treat headaches for over a hundred years in the United States and for much longer worldwide. Ergot medications are derived from rye and other grains, and they are used to treat cluster headaches as well as migraines. They work to block neurochemicals in the body, such as substance P, which act to either cause or worsen an already-present headache. The two key ergot oral medications used today to treat headaches are ergotamine tartrate and dihydroergotamine mesylate (DHE).

Ergot derivatives are available in sublingual (under the tongue) forms, as an intranasal spray (Migranal), and as rectal suppositories. Ergomar and Ergostat are the sublingual forms of the drug. In addition, ergotamine can be administered intravenously or subcutaneously (injected just under the skin). Caffeine is added to some preparations of ergotamine to speed up its delivery and action in the body.

Migranal is most effective when it's used in the prodrome stage of a migraine (characterized often as a generalized feeling of being somehow "off"). Since the oral form of the drug can cause nausea and vomiting, and many migraine patients are already nauseous to start with, patients with migraines should usually be given a non-oral form of ergotamine.

Ergotamines take action within about thirty to sixty minutes after taking them orally or rectally (and they act even faster if they are administered subcutaneously or intravenously), and the pain relief that they provide extends for about three to four hours.

Side Effects of Ergots

Ergot derivatives do have some side effects, including nausea and vomiting and anxiety; and these side effects are most prominent when the drug is given intravenously. A DHE nasal spray may sometimes cause nasal congestion. Frequent use of ergots may also lead to the development of a rebound headache.

Patients Who Should Avoid Ergots

Some patients should not take ergot derivatives, such as patients with high blood pressure (hypertension) or patients who either have—or think or know they're at risk for developing—heart disease. Any patients with circulatory problems (problems with the fluid circulation in their body) should avoid this medication. Also, those with a vasculitis process—a condition where the blood vessels are inflamed for any number of reasons—should not use medications in this class of drug. Pregnant women should definitely avoid this medication.

Muscle Relaxants: The Good and the Bad

Muscle relaxants are drugs that do just that: they relax the muscles. Sometimes painkillers are also prescribed along with muscle relaxants. Muscle relaxants can be used to treat chronic headaches, particularly cervicogenic headaches and tension-type headaches. They're generally ineffective in treating migraines, cluster headaches, and other headache types. Some examples of muscle relaxants are Soma or Sopridol (two forms of carisprodol), Flexeril (cyclobenzaprine), Skelaxin (metaxalone), and Robaxin (methocarbamol). These drugs are available in oral form, although some of them—such as methocarbamol—can also be injected.

Muscle relaxants usually cause sedation and they may also lead to impaired judgment while patients are under the influence of the medication. Patients who are already taking sedating drugs should avoid muscle relaxants. You should absolutely *not* drink any alcohol at all if you have taken a muscle relaxant—because the combination of the alcohol and the drug could cause a dangerously excessive sedation.

Another warning: if you take tricyclic antidepressants along with muscle relaxants, you risk an increase in side effects such as sedation. Other drugs to avoid when you take a muscle relaxant include antihistamines, sedatives, tranquilizers, narcotics, barbiturates, and anti-seizure medications. Also, never take more than one type of muscle relaxant at a time.

Patients with diabetes need to know that Skelaxin can cause a false elevated blood sugar reading. Muscle relaxants in general may cause such side effects as a rapid heartbeat, shortness of breath, skin rash, tightness in the chest, and stuffed up nose and reddened eyes. In addition, drugs in this class may cause blurred vision and unsteadiness in some patients.

Narcotics

Narcotics are drugs that the federal government has determined have a moderate to high risk of abuse or addiction, based on the Controlled Substances Act of 1990. They are also called "scheduled drugs." There are five schedules of narcotics, ranging from Schedule I—including the most addicting drugs—to Schedule V, or drugs that have some potential for abuse and addiction. All Schedule I drugs are illegal; and they include such drugs as heroin, "Ecstasy" (MDMA), peyote, and marijuana. Many narcotics used as pain remedies are Schedule II drugs.

Narcotics are carefully controlled by organizations like the Drug Enforcement Administration and other federal and state law enforcement organizations, because some people abuse or sell narcotics as well as abuse the medications that were legally prescribed to them by their doctors. If your doctor prescribes a narcotic for you but you find that it doesn't work well and you have some pills left, give them back to the doctor or throw them away. Never share your medications with others. It's illegal to even give away a narcotic medication. And don't keep them in your medicine cabinet either. Teenagers or others may find the drug and abuse it. Also, the efficacy of a drug erodes after a while, and a narcotic or other medication that you've had in your medicine cabinet for even one year may not be effective anymore. Or worse, the chemical composition of a medicine may change over time, particularly if left in a humid environment (like the bathroom medicine cabinet), and it may become dangerous to use.

Special Controls on Narcotics

As mentioned earlier, many narcotics are Schedule II drugs, and federal and state governments have placed special controls over them. For example, the doctor cannot call up a pharmacy to order a Schedule II drug over the telephone; instead, he must give the patient a written prescription for the medication. In addition, the prescription cannot be refilled; so if the patient needs more medication after a month, the doctor must write a new prescription.

Some examples of Schedule II drugs are OxyContin (a timed-release form of oxycodone), Percocet (oxycodone combined with acetaminophen), and Demerol (meperidine).

Narcotics Should Rarely Be the First Choice for Headache Pain

Narcotic painkillers are sometimes given to migraine patients or other patients with headaches who are in acute pain, especially when they are treated in the hospital emergency room. However, these drugs are usually *not* the best medications for patients with migraines or most other headache types. On occasion, while weighing the risks, benefits, and quality of life issues with the patient, we will allow some of our severe headache pain sufferers to use narcotic pain medication.

However, medication contracts with patients are needed, which are a signed agreement that a patient makes with the physician with regard to major rules that the physician sets about the use of narcotic medications. For example, the doctor may wish the patient to agree to obtain narcotics only from him and may stipulate that the patient agrees to random drug testing, as well as other provisions that the physician considers important. Frequent follow-up appointments and laboratory monitoring (including random urine drug testing) are all necessary components when using this class of medication.

In addition, narcotics are nearly always a bad idea for migraine patients who present with nausea and vomiting because they may increase the nausea that many migraine patients already suffer from. Also, if you suffer from chronic migraines, narcotics usually won't provide much relief. Remember the example of our patient in Chapter 4 who had been suffering from headaches for years and was taking narcotics for them but was still experiencing daily headaches? What she needed instead was surgery, not narcotics; and once she had her operation, her headaches went away.

At best, narcotic painkillers will drug the person into a dulled state where the pain is temporarily blocked; and at worst, the continuous use of narcotics can sometimes lead to a drug dependency.

If you do take narcotics for your pain, it's best to avoid taking them for longer than a few days or a week, unless the pain is extremely severe and other medications and procedures that have been attempted provide almost no relief.

Side Effects of Narcotics

Narcotics have many side effects but the primary ones are sedation, lethargy, dizziness, constipation, and the risk of developing an addiction to the drug. The addiction risk is not alarmingly high for most people who take the drug for pain rather than for recreational purposes, but it does exist. Patients who are taking narcotics should also avoid all alcohol, because the combination of the medication and the alcohol is potentially very dangerous and could even be fatal.

Patients who do become addicted to narcotics need medical supervision to taper off the drug and may need in-patient treatment.

Who Should Avoid Narcotics

Patients who have experienced a problem with alcohol and/or drug abuse in the past should avoid the chronic use of narcotics, because of their addictive potential. Most physicians are well aware of the risks that are associated with narcotics; however, patients who take narcotics should also educate themselves as much as possible about the drug. Patients who are taking other sedating medications should avoid narcotics unless their doctor recommends them.

Topical Prescribed Medications

Some medications can be introduced through the skin or the soft tissues and provide significant relief. For example, lidocaine can be used intranasally to treat an acute migraine attack. Using a swab, the lidocaine can be inserted inside the nose or on the outer part of it.

Lidoderm is a transdermal skin patch that delivers lidocaine to the skin for up to twelve hours. It may be particularly effective at treating patients who suffer from cervicogenic headaches, because the skin patches can be placed on the neck and/or the shoulders or upper spine, to provide anesthetic relief and subsequently may block headaches from developing in the first place.

Drugs such as lidocaine and Lidoderm usually have few side effects when used topically. I (Dr. Kandel), sometimes order the pharmacy to create a compound cream for my patients with cervicogenic headaches. It includes lidocaine and Orudis (ketoprofen)—an anti-inflammatory medication—and also Elavil (amitriptyline)—an antidepressant. Patients rub the cream on their necks four times a day.

Sometimes lidocaine or Lidoderm may cause a rash or skin irritation, in which case you should stop using the drug and tell your doctor about the problem. Patients who are allergic to lidocaine or other topical remedies should avoid the drug. However, most patients have no problem with lidocaine.

Butalbital (Fiornal, Fioricet)

Butalbital is a barbiturate and it's also another drug that's often used to treat tension-type and migraine headaches. The drug is usually included in combination with other medications. For example, Fiornal is a combination of butalbital, aspirin, and caffeine. In some cases, Fiornal also includes codeine, a narcotic. Fioricet is a combination of butalbital, acetaminophen, and caffeine.

Barbiturates such as butalbital are Schedule III drugs, which means that they have a lower potential for abuse and addiction than the Schedule II drugs discussed earlier in this chapter (such as Percocet and OxyContin). As a result, the law allows doctors to call in a prescription for drugs in this category, and they may also give medication refills to patients.

Side Effects of Butalbital

With frequent use of butalbital, patients with chronic headaches are at risk of developing rebound headaches. As a result, most physicians discourage the chronic or frequent use of these drugs and instead, use them only as a backup medication when other drugs are not available.

Butalbital can also affect sleep. According to Dr. Silberstein and Dr. McCrory in their 2001 article for *Headache*, the drug can decrease slow-wave sleep and may cause mood changes, impaired judgment, and an impairment of fine motor skills. In some cases, butalbital can also cause an intoxication that is indistinguishable from alcohol abuse. In addition, butalbital can cause addiction in some patients. As a result, some patients who take butalbital may take a pill even when they don't have a headache because they worry that they might get one if they don't take the drug. This counterproductive behavior contributes to the development of rebound headaches.

Withdrawal from Butalbital

Patients who are addicted to butalbital will experience withdrawal symptoms if they stop taking the drug. In the case of barbiturates such as butalbital, the symptoms of withdrawal may occur in eight to thirty-six hours after the last dosage was taken; and they may last from two to fifteen days. During withdrawal from butalbital, patients may experience nausea and vomiting, dizziness, weight loss, low blood pressure, and even seizures.

If you take butalbital on a regular basis, don't just stop taking the drug without talking to your doctor about it. He may advise that you taper off the drug and/or prescribe other medications—such as a low dose of phenobarbital—that can help you through a washout of the drug from your system.

Specialized Migraine Medications: The Triptans

When it was first approved by the Food and Drug Administration (FDA) in 1993, Imitrex (sumatriptan) was a godsend to most people with chronic migraines. It worked far more rapidly to combat migraine pain than any other drug that was previously available; and if Imitrex was taken at the initial onset of a migraine, it could often stop the headache cold in its tracks. Many patients still receive good pain relief from Imitrex, particularly from the subcutaneous injection.

However, since the approval of Imitrex, newer "triptan" medications—all selective serotonin agonists—have been developed. Other triptans that may be prescribed in the United States as of this writing include Zomig (zolmitriptan), Amerge (naratriptan), Maxalt (rizatriptan), Axert (almotriptan), Frova (frovatriptan), and Relpax (eletriptan). Of these drugs, injected Imitrex is still the fastest, acting within fifteen minutes. The other medications may take between twenty minutes to an hour or more to act.

This would make many readers think that they should inevitably use Imitrex over all other triptans, since it's the fastest acting; and it often *is* a good choice. However, Imitrex doesn't work well for everyone and sometimes another triptan is effective when Imitrex fails. As a result, don't give up altogether on triptans as a class of drugs unless you've tried every available brand.

In general, it's best to give a triptan at least two or three trials before giving up on it and asking your doctor for a different triptan. And keep in mind that sometimes your headaches may not be migraines at all. Instead, you may be suffering from cervicogenic headaches or another form of headaches; and triptans are specifically designed for migraineurs.

Side Effects and Who Should Avoid Triptans

Although not common, the repeated use of triptan medications can lead to the development of rebound headaches in some patients. Some patients may experience dizziness, drowsiness, nausea, and weakness from triptans.

Patients with coronary artery disease or uncontrolled high blood pressure should not take any triptan medication because the drugs may aggravate the coronary artery syndrome in patients with already-existing disease.

Another precaution: patients who are also taking antidepressants in the serotonin reuptake inhibitor class (such as Prozac or Zoloft) and who take a triptan drug may develop something called *serotonin syndrome*. This is a dangerous condition that can lead to tremors, shivering, restlessness, mood changes, and other side effects requiring emergency medical care.

In general, many patients should have no problem with triptan medications. In fact, according to an article on "migraine headache misconceptions" in a 2004 issue of *Pharmacotherapy*, it's a myth that triptans could induce cardiac illness and even death. According to the authors, in defending the use of triptans for migraines, withholding them from patients because of a fear of heart problems is not justified. Say the authors, "The lone exception to our statement is the unlikely individual with migraine who is at high risk for cardiovascular events; nearly 75 percent of all migraineurs are women younger than 45 years, a group for whom multiple cardiovascular risk factors are uncommon."

Medications for Nausea and Vomiting

Because so many patients with chronic migraines experience nausea and vomiting, they may need antiemetic drugs such as Reglan (metoclopramide), Compazine (prochlorperazine), and either Phenergan or Promethegan (both are brand names of promethazine). These medications often help control nausea and vomiting, and they also provide pain relief. However, doctors warn against the chronic use of these drugs because frequent use of antiemetics may cause liver disease, blood abnormalities, and other medical problems. Sedation is a major concern with antiemetics, but sedation can also lead to a rapid resolution of the nausea.

Some patients have found relief from the severe nausea associated with their migraines with a form of Valium (diazepam) called Diastat. This medication comes in a syringe with two to a pack. It is injected rectally but there are no needles! Diastat may be more sedating than other forms of antiemetics.

Newer Medication Solutions Given to Prevent Headaches

Because prevention is important to people with chronic headaches, many patients seek medications that can help them with this goal. Topamax (topiramate) is a promising medication that has been approved by the FDA to treat migraines. Topamax is an anti-seizure drug, but it has proved very effective among patients with migraines and other chronic headaches. Medications in the beta blocker or calcium channel blocker class may also be effective in preventing headaches in some patients. In addition, some patients with chronic migraines or tension-type headaches may improve with low dosages of antidepressants.

Side Effects of Topamax

In addition to "pins and needles," fatigue, and diarrhea, patients taking Topamax on a regular basis could develop kidney stones and should therefore be sure to drink plenty of fluid as a preventive measure. In addition, if you experience any eye pain while taking Topamax, stop taking the drug and call your doctor, because rarely it is associated with the development of glaucoma.

Some patients complain that Topamax makes their memory more fuzzy than usual. They may also experience nausea; and in a few cases the drug causes food to taste differently, which has led patients to discontinue its use. One side effect that most patients like is that Topamax may cause weight loss, although this effect doesn't occur for everyone.

One precaution should be noted: Topamax may make oral contraception less effective, so alternative forms of birth control should be practiced if you take this medication and need contraceptive protection. While studies indicate that this problem is more common at higher doses (100–200 mg per day), a bit of caution is advised at all doses.

A Study Conducted to Test the Effectiveness of Topamax

In a study in the 2004 issue of the *Journal of the American Medical Association* (*JAMA*), patients with a history of migraine were assigned to 50 mg, 100 mg, or 200 mg of Topamax; or they received the placebo drug. The patients were started at the lowest dosage of the medication according to the group they were randomly assigned to, which was then increased by 25 mg per week. The researchers concluded that Topamax is effective in treating migraines in the first month of treatment.

The average number of headaches decreased from 5.4 per month to 4.1 for patients taking 50 mg of Topamax. A better improvement was seen with patients taking 100 mg, and patients in this group experienced an average decrease from 5.8 headaches to 3.5 headaches a month. The patients taking 200 mg of Topamax had the best response and went from an average of 5.1 headaches to 3.0 headaches per month. In contrast, the patients who took a placebo improved slightly, from 5.6 migraines a month to 4.5 headaches. Clearly, the Topamax was helpful to the migraine patients.

Some patients in the study experienced side effects that led to their withdrawal from treatment, such as "pins and needles" (paresthesias), fatigue, appetite loss, weight loss, and diarrhea. Some patients also experienced memory problems when they took 100 mg and greater dosages.

Other Anti-Seizure Medications

There are other anticonvulsant drugs that are also used to treat chronic headache sufferers. Depakote and Depakote ER are anti-convulsants that have been approved by the Food and Drug Administration to treat migraines. However, these drugs have major side effects, such as a severe weight gain (up to fifty pounds). They may also cause pancreatitis, a painful swelling of the pancreas. Other side effects are nausea and vomiting, sedation, and tremor.

Beta Blockers

Some patients who have chronic headaches as well as high blood pressure may benefit from taking a medication in the beta-blocker class as a preventive drug against headaches. Inderal (propranolol) and Timolide (timolol) are commonly prescribed beta blockers. Some other beta blockers include Corgard (nadolol), Lopressor and Toprol-XL (two brand names of metoprolol), and Tenormin (atenolol). Keep in mind, however, that the chronic use of beta blockers can sometimes lead to the development of rebound headaches.

Beta blockers can also cause side effects such as weight gain, dizziness, gastrointestinal disorders, and impotence, to name just a few. A slower than normal pulse, often associated with near fainting (syncope), can be seen with these drugs. Of course, some people experience many side effects, while others have a few, and still others have none at all.

Headache patients with diabetes, depression, asthma, or heart disease should avoid beta blockers. In addition, patients over age 65 should check with their family physician before using beta blockers because these medications have been shown to be associated with cognitive slowing and memory loss in senior adults.

Calcium Channel Blockers

Patients with frequent headaches may be given calcium channel blockers to help prevent headaches, especially migraines and cluster headaches. It is believed that calcium channel blockers may affect the neurotransmitters that are commonly associated with migraines. Calan, Isoptin, and Verelan (which are all different brand names of verapamil) are common calcium channel blockers that are used in patients with migraines as well as patients with frequent cluster headaches.

Note: Medications in the calcium channel blocker class should not be used together with beta blocker medications.

Calcium channel blockers can cause some aggravating side effects, including low blood pressure, dizziness, and constipation. Patients who are pregnant as well as patients with low blood pressure should avoid this class of drugs. In addition, if you have a history of heart disease, stay away from calcium channel blockers. Calcium channel blockers are generally not recommended for patients with Parkinson's disease.

Antidepressants

Many patients are surprised and sometimes even offended when their doctor suggests that they take an antidepressant for chronic headaches. Yet antidepressants, particularly those in the tricyclic class, have been shown to be effective in treating some headache patients. Some tricyclic antidepressants are stimulating, such as Vivactil (protriptyline), and Pamelor and Aventyl (two brand names of nortriptyline), while others are sedating, such as Elavil (amitriptyline).

Tricyclic antidepressants, such as Elavil, can cause weight gain, urinary retention, dry mouth and dry eye, constipation, sedation, and chronic tiredness. Selective serotonin reuptake inhibitor (SSRI) antidepressants such as Prozac (fluoxetine) and Zoloft (sertraline) can cause dizziness, insomnia, and tremors. Effexor (venlafaxine) is another example of an SSRI that is sometimes used to treat chronic headaches.

Some patients should avoid tricyclic antidepressants altogether, particularly those with glaucoma, low blood pressure, and a preexisting problem with urinary retention.

In Table 10.1, we provide a quick summary of the medications that can help with particular types of headaches, grouping them by drug category, and including their brand and generic name.

TABLE 10.1 Common Medications Used to Treat Headaches

Drug Category	Brand (Generic)	Type of Headache
Triptans	Imitrex (sumatriptan)	Migraine
	Zomig (zolmitriptan)	
	Maxalt (rizatriptan)	
	Axert (almotriptan)	
	Frova (frovatriptan)	
	Relpax (eletriptan)	
NSAIDs	Anaprox (naproxen sodium)	Cervicogenic/ Tension-Type
	Orudis (ketoprofen)	
	Feldene (piroxicam)	
	Clinoril (sulindac)	
	Relafen (nabumetone)	
	Anaprox, Naprosyn (naproxen sodium)	
	Tolectin (tolmetin sodium)	
	Mobic (meloxicam)	
Muscle relaxants	Skelaxin (metaxalone)	Cervicogenic/Tension-Type
	Soma or Sopridol (two forms of carisprodol)	
	Flexeril (cyclobenzaprine)	
	Robaxin (methocarbamol)	
Ergotamine	Ergomar and Ergostat (sublingual ergotamine)	Cluster/Migraine
	Migranal (nasal ergotamine)	
	Ergotamine tartrate	
	Dihydroergotamine mesylate (DHE)	
Anti-seizure	Topamax (topiramate)	Migraine/Tension-Type/ Cluster
Barbiturates	Fioricet (butalbital)	Tension-Type/Cervicogenic
	Fiornal (butalbital combinations)	
Antidepressants	Elavil (amitriptyline)	All Headaches
	Pamelor and Aventyl (two brand names of nortriptyline)	
Selective Serotonin Reuptake Inhibitors	Effexor (venlafaxine)	All Headaches
	Zoloft (sertraline)	
Beta Blockers	Corgard (nadolol)	Migraines
	Lopressor and Toprol-XL (brand names of metoprolol)	
	Tenormin (atenolol)	

TABLE 10.1 Common Medications Used to Treat Headaches,
continued

Calcium Channel Blockers	Calan, Isoptin, and Verelan (brand names of verapamil)	Cluster/Migraines
Narcotics*	Percocet (oxycodone and acetaminophen)	Migraines
	OxyContin (time-released oxycodone)	
	Vicodin (hydrocodone and acetaminophen)	
	Lortab (hydrocodone with acetaminophen)	
	Demerol (meperidine)	
Antiemetics (antinausea)	Reglan (metoclopramide)	Migraines/Cluster
	Compazine (prochlorperazine)	
	Phenergan and Promethegan (brand names of promethazine)	
	Diastat (diazepam)	
Local Anesthetic Cream	Topical lidocaine	Tension-Type/Cervicogenic
Topical Anesthetic	Lidoderm	Cervicogenic
	Lidocaine (intranasal)	Cluster

*We do not recommend narcotics for most headaches.

This chapter covered prescribed medications used to treat chronic severe headaches. But the majority of patients actually rely upon OTC medications and/or supplements to cope with their headaches. The next chapter provides you with the information you need to know on these topics.

11

Over-the-Counter Drugs, Vitamins, and Supplements

Many people think that only prescribed medications are strong enough to beat back their severe headaches. And it's often true that you *do* need to take a prescription drug when you're in the agonizing throes of a five-alarm headache. But there are also other medications that may help you control your headache pain, such as aspirin, Tylenol (acetaminophen), and ibuprofen, the ones with which we're all most familiar. In addition, sometimes supplements of minerals, vitamins, or other substances may help you in cutting back the number and/or intensity of your headaches. For example, supplements such as magnesium, vitamin B_2, or melatonin, may be particularly effective for chronic headache sufferers, especially if you suffer from migraines or cluster headaches. At the same time, there are also risks associated with the frequent use of OTC remedies for headaches, as well as risks associated with taking supplements.

Tom suffered from frequent headaches, so he took Tylenol nearly every day. Tom is also what he calls a social drinker and enjoys three or four shots of bourbon, pretty much every night. When we told him that his liver was inflamed, and this was a serious problem, Tom was shocked. Apparently the combination of the frequent use of Tylenol and alcohol had led to the liver inflammation. Fortunately for Tom, we discovered the problem in time. Upon our urging, Tom quit drinking altogether and we took him off all Tylenol as well. After several months, Tom's liver recovered. In addition, Tom's frequent headaches were gone. Now, if he developed a headache, he limited himself to only one regular-strength tablet, as we recommended.

In Tom's case, it was probably his frequent drinking that contributed to his headaches, but you could be a person who never drinks and OTC remedies and supplements still hold both benefits and risks for you. This chapter offers important information on the pros and cons of OTC drugs and supplements for headache sufferers.

The Old Standbys: Tylenol, Excedrin, and Aspirin

Many people rely upon over-the-counter (OTC) drugs like Tylenol, ibuprofen, and aspirin to relieve their headache pain as well as other aches and pains they suffer from, such as arthritic pain. After all, when you have pain, isn't this type of drug usually effective? Yes it is; and when these drugs are used only occasionally most people will be fine. In fact, one baby aspirin a day has been shown to reduce the risk of strokes in many people. However, the chronic use of these seemingly innocuous drugs can be dangerously unhealthy.

What's Good About Them

The benefits of such OTC headache remedies as aspirin, acetaminophen, and ibuprofen are clearly evident. They're generally inexpensive, you can buy them at virtually any supermarket or convenience store, and you don't have to see a doctor beforehand to obtain a prescription for them. OTC medications also generally work fairly rapidly—if they do work for you. There's also no social stigma to taking OTC drugs, and you won't become addicted to them. (However, some people do develop rebound headaches from the frequent use of some OTC drugs, such as over-the-counter NSAIDs, like ibuprofen.)

Concerns About Over-the-Counter NSAIDs

As mentioned earlier, it has been known for some time that the chronic use of nonsteroidal inflammatory medications (NSAIDs), whether prescribed or over-the-counter, can cause ulcers and gastrointestinal bleeding. Like the concerns of prescription COX-2 inhibitors and some of the other NSAIDs showing a risk for heart disease, some studies have also shown that patients who frequently use prescribed or over-the-counter NSAIDs may have an increased risk for cardiovascular disease, including heart attack and stroke. As a result, in 2005 the FDA requested that the manufacturers of both over-the-counter and prescribed NSAIDs revise their labels to include warning information on possible cardiovascular risks with the use of these medications. Manufacturers of products containing ibuprofen (Advil, Motrin, and other brands), naproxen (Aleve) and ketoprofen (Orudis, Actron) have had to revise their labeling to include information about which patients should consult with their doctors before using these medications.

Patients who know or suspect that they may be at risk for cardiovascular disease (people who have had a heart attack or stroke, have heart disease, or have a close family member—such as a parent or sibling—who has had a heart attack or stroke) should discuss with their physicians whether or not they should use NSAIDs. In addition, patients over the age of 65 should be informed of the possible increased risk of heart attack or stroke, because aging increases the risk for cardiovascular events such as these. For their own safety, patients who are not sure if they are at risk for cardiovascular disease should consult their physicians before taking any over-the-counter NSAIDs.

What's Bad About Them

Now for the bad side of these OTC headache remedies. As with Tom at the beginning of this chapter, the frequent use of Tylenol can damage your liver and even lead to liver cirrhosis (severe inflammation). This is true even if you don't drink alcohol at all, although alcohol makes the situation worse. You only have one liver, and you need it to survive. If your liver fails, then the only other option that's left is a liver transplant. Tylenol is also dangerous if you already have kidney or liver disease, and in those cases, the drug should be avoided altogether.

Your liver and kidneys aren't the only organs that can develop damage from the chronic use of OTC drugs for headaches. OTC nonsteroidal anti-inflammatory drugs (NSAIDs) such as ibuprofen and aspirin may relieve headache pain; but they may also erode the sensitive lining of the stomach, and as a result, frequent use can lead to potentially life-threatening gastrointestinal bleeding and even the development of gastric ulcers. Be sure to avoid taking diuretics (water pills) when you're also taking NSAIDs, because diuretics can increase your risk for developing kidney and liver problems. If you take diuretics and then add an NSAID on a regular basis, you further accelerate your risk.

NSAIDs also interact with many other drugs, particularly anti-seizure medications, gout medications, hypertension drugs, antidiabetic medications, heart medications, and beta blockers. If you're taking a medication that is in any of these classes, do *not* take any NSAIDs, including aspirin or ibuprofen, unless you check with your doctor first.

Supplements That May Help You

Although many doctors are wary of patients who load up on large quantities of supplements that they buy in their local health food store or the supermarket, some research is showing a valid use for some supplements taken by headache sufferers, especially among individuals who have chronic migraine headaches or cluster headaches. This is especially true in the case of several specific supplements, including magnesium, melatonin, riboflavin (vitamin B_2), and coenzyme Q10.

Considering Magnesium

The magnesium levels in your blood may be too low, and if so, one of your symptoms will be a severe headache, particularly a migraine, a cluster headache, or a menstrual migraine. You may also be borderline-low and still suffer from frequent headaches that may improve with taking magnesium supplements.

Why do people become deficient in magnesium? *Hypomagnesia* (a condition of below-normal levels of magnesium in your blood) may be caused by taking diuretics (water pills). You may also be at risk for hypomagnesia if you have diabetes that is not under control. Heavy drinkers may develop hypomagnesia (yet another reason to curtail drinking!), as may patients taking some anti-cancer drugs, such as Cisplatin. In addition, if you've recently had a very severe bout with the flu, including such symptoms as lots of diarrhea and vomiting, then you may be at least a little deficient in magnesium until your body recovers.

Some people develop chronic headaches because of magnesium deficiencies, especially women. For many people with chronic headaches, particularly migraines, low doses of magnesium supplements can help to reduce the frequency and intensity of their headaches. The downside is that magnesium often causes stomach upset and temporary diarrhea. However, if you're a person who's chronically constipated, magnesium might give you the additional advantage of helping to make you "regular," in addition to blocking headache formation.

Warning: Be sure that you talk to your doctor before you start taking magnesium. It's dangerous to take magnesium to excess and could lead to a condition called *hypermagnesia* (too much magnesium in your blood). People who rely heavily on laxatives with magnesium are also at risk for this condition.

You can also enhance your intake by eating foods that are rich in magnesium, and there are many of them, such as bananas, whole wheat bread, potatoes, shredded wheat cereal, cashews, peanuts, and shrimp—just to name a few very diverse items.

Studies to Investigate the Effectiveness of Magnesium in Treating Migraines

In the case of acute migraines, magnesium sulfate may be given intravenously by physicians, although this is not a standard therapy. In a study reported in *Headache* in 2000, 15 patients with severe migraines were given magnesium intravenously and the pain disappeared altogether in 13 of them (87 percent). Of course, you can't have magnesium intravenously every time you get a migraine, but some experts believe that supplemental magnesium that's taken orally may also help some patients to stave off their migraines.

Another study on the use of magnesium (in *Cephalgia* in 1996) indicated that taking supplements of magnesium reduced the intensity and duration of migraine headaches for some migraineurs, although it did not cut back on the number of headaches that they experienced. So they still had about the same number of headaches, but these headaches hurt less and lasted for a shorter period. Not as good as a total cure, but an improvement nonetheless.

Magnesium deficiency may also be the cause for menstrual migraines, and in a study reported in 2002 in *Headache*, the researchers checked the blood of 270 women of childbearing age for an ionized magnesium deficiency. The researchers found that among some women, their magnesium levels were significantly low during their menstrual periods. For example, among women who had migraines during their periods, 45 percent of them were deficient in magnesium. In looking at women who had migraines when they did *not* have their periods, only 15 percent were deficient in magnesium. Apparently menstruation increased the risk for magnesium deficiency among some women, which in turn increased the risk for getting a migraine.

Further studies need to be done but it seems logical to assume that magnesium, menstruation, and migraines are all tied together.

Feverfew

A lot of so-called alternative remedies are nonsense, particularly the many drugs that purport to help you lose a great deal of weight very fast. But there are a few herbal remedies that have been anecdotally shown to be effective at combating severe head-aches—although clinical studies have not backed up their effectiveness. Feverfew is one such remedy.

While studies have not indicated that feverfew effectively combats headaches, many people with migraines insist that taking feverfew has improved their condition. This may be a placebo effect (which means that people think it'll work and this belief causes it to work for them), or feverfew may actually help with migraines. Researchers have not yet discovered if, how, and why feverfew may be effective.

If you decide to try feverfew, keep in mind that supporters say that the full effect won't be gained for at least a few weeks. As far as we know, there aren't any foods you can eat to increase your feverfew level. You actually have to take feverfew supplements to determine if it helps you or not. Keep in mind that feverfew is, as are many other supplements, poorly standardized; and you can never really know how much or how little of the active ingredient you are actually getting.

Melatonin

Some studies have shown that supplemental melatonin may be preventive against headaches, particularly cluster headaches and migraines. If your headaches stem from chronic sleep deprivation, taking melatonin for a short period (such as a week) may help you to reset your disordered sleep cycle. (Some patients may need to take melatonin for weeks or months before they see results.)

In many cases, the headache problem may be linked to a sleep disorder and/or a disruption in the patient's sleep-wake cycle. Frankly, in our busy world, it's very easy to develop a sleep disorder; and many people stay awake at night, worrying about their life problems. This insomnia further increases the risk for headaches and other health problems. It's a vicious cycle and supplemental melatonin may help you to break out of it.

The pineal gland actually produces natural melatonin; and its primary purpose appears to be to maintain your normal sleep-wake cycle, or what some experts call the circadian rhythm. Experts believe that the circadian rhythm of people with cluster headaches may be unstable, and they point to the fact that most cluster headache sufferers develop these headaches at night. Some studies with a small number of subjects have shown that supplemental melatonin has significantly decreased the number of cluster headaches, while other studies have not found any significant improvement with melatonin.

Melatonin may also be effective in preventing migraines. A study reported in *Neurology* in 2004 indicated that melatonin was effective at migraine prevention in many of the subjects. Of 32 subjects, 25 of them (78 percent) experienced a 50 percent or greater reduction in their headache frequency after taking melatonin supplements. None of the patients had an increase in the number of their headaches. Dramatically, eight patients experienced a complete recovery from their migraines after taking melatonin.

As far as we know, there are no foods that contain melatonin. However, if your main problem is insomnia, which may be causing or contributing to your headaches, then you might consider eating some foods with soporific qualities, such as turkey or milk.

Coenzyme Q10

Coenzyme Q10 is a biologically active chemical that facilitates many important metabolic functions. Supplementation with this chemical frequently leads to a reduction of migraine frequency and severity. Coenzyme Q10 has been studied in mainstream medical trials (such as reported in *Cephalgia* in 2002), and has been shown to be effective at a dose of 150 mg a day. No data supports the use of this supplement for other headache types; but in some cases of migraine headaches, the results can be amazing. This compound is readily available in supermarkets and health food stores.

Riboflavin (Vitamin B$_2$)

In one study, reported in a 2004 issue of *Headache*, the researchers studied two groups of patients. One group (the study group) received a large dose of riboflavin (400 mg), along with magnesium (300 mg), and feverfew (100 mg). The other group, the placebo group, received only a low dose of riboflavin (25 mg). The study included 49 patients who were studied over three months.

The results were quite unexpected. The placebo group reported a marked remission of their headaches, as did the study group. For example, success was defined as a 50 percent or greater decrease in the number of migraines, and this result occurred in 42 percent of the study patients who received the riboflavin, magnesium, and feverfew; and in 44 percent of the patients who received only the riboflavin. Both groups also experienced fewer migraine days. The common denominator in both groups was the riboflavin. Although further studies are needed, it appears that a low dose of riboflavin may help some patients with chronic headaches.

A change in diet might also help. Some foods that are rich in riboflavin are:

- Milk
- Yogurt
- Cheese
- Eggs
- Nuts
- Lean meats
- Most cereals (check the nutrition label on the package)

Suggestions for Buying OTC Vitamins and Supplements

If you decide to purchase vitamins or other supplements such as magnesium, feverfew, or melatonin (sometimes called "nutraceuticals") from a retail store or over the Internet, we are including some important cautions for you to consider. The reason for this is that many people assume that the Food and Drug Administration (FDA) or another government agency closely oversees and monitors all vitamins, minerals, and herbal remedies that are sold to consumers. This is simply not true.

Instead, supplements and herbal remedies fall under the rule of the Dietary Supplement and Health Education Act, a law that was enacted by Congress in 1994. As a result, these products are not required to be subjected to the rigorous testing that the FDA demands in the case of prescribed drugs or even OTC drugs such as acetaminophen, aspirin, or ibuprofen. It is also more difficult for the FDA to pull supplements or herbal remedies off the market than it is for them to ban prescribed drugs or OTC drugs.

Here are our carefully considered recommendations for you. Please read them before you buy any vitamins, supplements, or herbal remedies for your headaches.

Tip 1: Buy Products Manufactured in the United States or Canada

Sometimes products are manufactured in other countries and then are distributed in the United States or Canada. This is not good enough. The products should be made in northern America. The reason for this is that medical journal studies have found that some products produced in other countries have been adulterated with mercury, arsenic, lead, testosterone, and other substances that you shouldn't consume.

Tip 2: When Buying over the Internet, Check the Origin of the Vendor

If you decide to buy a product over the Internet (you should be able to buy most products locally, but we realize this isn't always possible), do not buy anything unless you can find a U.S. or Canadian address on the website. The reason for this is that sometimes sellers may try to conceal that they are located in another country by leaving out their address.

Often you can find this address by looking on the website for a place to click on, such as "Contact Us." Other times, the address is plainly visible on the home page. When you can't find an address, then go to another site. If you do find an address, then check further that the product is manufactured in the United States or Canada. If that information is unavailable, send an e-mail to the company and ask them where the product is made, not distributed.

Tip 3: When Buying in a Store, Check the Label

If you're in a store considering whether to buy a product, check the label to see all the ingredients that the product is made of. Maybe you need only magnesium or only feverfew, but the product also includes many items that aren't necessary for you.

In the case of feverfew, however, the package may give you percentage or other information on its parthenolide content. Parthenolide is the substance within feverfew that purportedly helps people with migraines, because of its anti-inflammatory properties. So if parthenolide is listed on the label, that's okay.

Tip 4: Pay Attention to the Dosage

Ask your doctor what dose to take of the vitamin or supplement. If he isn't sure, check the product label and take the lowest possible dose. Do not assume that if the label says to take one pill or capsule, you should take two since your headache is really awful. This is a bad mistake!

If there are competing companies selling different dosages, buy the one that offers the lowest dosage. If the lower dosage doesn't work for you, your doctor may want you to take a higher dosage—but ask first.

Tip 5: Watch for Side Effects

Stop taking the product if it causes any distressing side effects, such as nausea and vomiting or severe diarrhea. (Magnesium supplements can cause loose stools but should not cause severe diarrhea unless an excessive dosage is taken.) Tell your doctor what happened. Don't be embarrassed or afraid that your physician will criticize you for taking a supplement on your own. Doctors know that many people buy vitamins and supplements to try to feel better. Even if your doctor does yell at you (which is unlikely), it's better that he knows what is going on so that he can advise you of what to do next.

Tip 6: Compare Prices

Consider how many pills or capsules are in a container first to determine the real price of the product. The one that seems the most inexpensive can sometimes be the priciest when you don't consider the number of pills inside the container. You don't even have to leave the store to do a price comparison, because many stores sell the same product (such as magnesium, feverfew, or vitamin B_2) manufactured and packaged by several competitors.

Take a calculator with you and do the math. In a hypothetical example, one container of the product that you want may sell 60 capsules for $10.00, which is about 17 cents each. Another container may have 35 tablets for $7.99, which is about 23 cents each. In this case, the higher-priced product is a better deal—as long as it wasn't manufactured outside the U.S. or Canada. (Remember our first caution to you in this list.)

Tip 7: Talk with Your Physician

Be sure to tell your doctor if you plan to take (or have already started taking) any herbs, supplements, or OTC drugs. Some herbs can have a very dangerous interaction with other medications that you take. For example, if you take Coumadin (warfarin), a blood thinner, you should never take vitamin E, because you could cause your blood to become too thin.

Alcohol and Medication Interactions

This section may seem odd here, but we are including it because although many people are careful about avoiding alcohol when they take narcotics or many other prescribed drugs, they think nothing of having a few drinks while also taking acetaminophen, ibuprofen, or aspirin. Yes, these are all OTC drugs that each have dangerous interactions.

Of course, if you have chronic headaches, you should avoid alcohol in any form. First of all, alcohol can trigger headaches in some people, even if it's only a glass of wine that is consumed. Secondly, alcohol interacts with most medications, including most OTC drugs. You'll increase your risk of gastrointestinal bleeding when you combine alcohol with a NSAID. So don't imagine that aspirin and other OTC remedies are invariably safe and would never hurt you. Used frequently, they can do a lot of damage to the body. You should also avoid alcohol if you're taking any herbal remedies, such as chamomile, valerian, echinacea, or melatonin. These remedies are sometimes taken by people with insomnia, but alcohol further increases the drowsiness that is associated with them.

We've provided you with a quick reference (Table 11.1) so you can easily see how some common prescription and OTC medica-

TABLE 11.1 Common Prescribed and Over-the-Counter Medications and Supplements That May Interact with Alcohol

Drug Class	Generic (Brand) Name	Availability	Type of Reaction
Analgesics	Aspirin, acetaminophen (various brands, Tylenol)	Rx and OTC	Increases gastric emptying, leading to faster alcohol absorption in the small intestine. Alcohol enhances acetaminophen metabolism and may cause liver damage.
NSAIDs	Ibuprofen (Motrin and various brands), Ketoprofen (Orudis), Naproxen (Naprosyn, Anaprox), Diclofenac (Voltaren)	Rx and OTC	Alcohol consumption increases the risk of gastrointestinal bleeding.
Herbal Medications (Sleep aids)	Valerian, Melatonin	Chamomile, Echinacea, OTC	Alcohol may accentuate drowsiness associated with these supplements.

Source: This material was adapted from the table "Interactions Between Alcohol and Various Classes of Medications," in "Alcohol and Medication Interactions," *Alcohol Research & Health* 23, no. 1, 1999.

tions and supplements can interact with alcohol. However, this list is not inclusive. There are numerous prescribed and OTC medications that interact with alcohol; and this chart only provides a small sampling of drugs that may be dangerous when taken with alcohol. For example, narcotics should never be taken in conjunction with alcohol, nor should any drugs with sedating effects.

Now that you have explored the various prescription and over-the-counter treatment options, look at the next chapter on Botox therapy (which benefits many headache patients).

CHAPTER 12

Botox: A New Biologic Drug for Pain

Botox is no longer just a cosmetic drug for aging movie stars, politicians, or others who decide that they need their facial wrinkles ironed out. Or, as one physician put it, "We use Botox for pain, not for 'vain.'" Many doctors are now using Botox therapy to treat a variety of painful conditions in their patients, including the pain of chronic severe headaches. We have used Botox successfully on some of our own headache patients, and have been very impressed with the results.

Diana, 37, had been suffering from severe headaches for years when she first came to our office, and her headaches occurred 3–4 days each week. She took Fioricet for pain; and if it got really bad, switched to Percocet, a stronger narcotic. The drugs diminished her pain, but she complained that they made her feel dopey and tired—especially the Percocet. After a thorough physical examination and a review of her laboratory tests and X-rays, I (Dr. Kandel) diagnosed Diana with a cervicogenic headache with spasm of the neck muscles and told her that I thought Botox might help.

My office checked with her insurance company and after one initial denial and an appeal, they agreed to provide coverage for Botox. (If your insurance company doesn't agree to cover the cost of Botox or if you have no insurance, keep reading. There are programs you may be eligible for that may provide free Botox, discussed later in this chapter.)

We arranged for a later appointment, and when she came in, I injected Diana in the forehead and neck areas where her pain predominated. She felt a little better right away. Diana called me a week later and told me it was a miracle! No headaches at all! She said, "This Botox stuff is definitely a keeper!" When I saw Diana in the office four weeks after the injections, she told me that she had experienced two mild headaches since I had injected the Botox, and they were so mild that she didn't take any medicine for them.

So, bottom line, Diana was down from 12–16 severe headaches a month to only 2 mild headaches. About three months after the first injections, her chronic headaches started to come back, so I gave Diana another series of Botox shots. After that, she was fine for five months before she called me again and said she needed more injections.

What *Is* Botox?

Botulinum toxin type A, or "Botox," the brand name used by Allergan, Inc. (the sole provider of botulinum toxin type A in the United States), is actually a protein made by *Clostridium botulinum*. *Clostridia* are bacteria that you don't want in your digestive system because if they somehow *did* get into your stomach and colon, you'd become very sick with food poisoning. But when the treated and purified toxin that *Clostridium* makes is injected into your tensed muscles (assuming that the treatment is effective for you), it works very well to relax the overstretched muscles that were the cause of so much pain and improves blood flow to the area—another pain reducer. Botox is chemically purified and contains no actual bacteria; so you can't get botulism (food poisoning) from a Botox injection.

In 1989, Botox was first approved by the Food and Drug Administration (FDA) as a treatment for facial spastic disorders. In

2000, the FDA approved Botox as a therapy for *cervical dystonia*, a neck spasm disorder. It was also approved in 2000 as a therapy for the cosmetic treatment of facial wrinkles, although many doctors had used the drug for this purpose for years before then. As of this writing, Botox is not officially approved by the FDA for the treatment of headaches; however, clinical studies performed by physicians have proven it effective in headache treatment for many patients, and we have also found it effective in many of our own patients.

The use of Botox for headaches was discovered accidentally by William Binder, a California otolaryngologist (ear, nose, and throat doctor) in 1992 when he was using Botox for cosmetic purposes, to rid patients of facial wrinkles. So many patients told him that their migraines had resolved that Dr. Binder realized that Botox could be an effective preventive therapy for headaches. Since then, thousands of headache patients have found that Botox works for them too. (Dr. Binder even went so far as to obtain a usage patent on Botox for migraines.)

Botox won't work well on every form of headache but does seem effective in a variety of headaches, including migraines and cervicogenic headaches. Some studies have also shown Botox to be effective in patients with "whiplash" injuries that were sustained in car accidents. However, Botox won't work for the sinus headache; and in our practice, has not been shown to be effective with chronic cluster headaches.

How Does Botox Work?

Experts disagree on specifically *how* Botox works. They know that it blocks the production of acetylcholine, a chemical necessary for muscle contraction, and some experts believe that stopping acetylcholine cold is the key to its success in pain elimination or reduction. Botox also inhibits the production of other pain-generating chemicals in the body, such as "substance P," a neuro-

Clinical Study Supports Botox Therapy for Chronic Headache Pain

In one study, 271 headache patients received Botox therapy for an average of about nine months each; and the results of their experiences were reported in a 2003 issue of *Headache*. Of these patients most had chronic daily headaches (57 percent), followed by mixed headaches (26 percent), migraines (11 percent), and tension-type headaches (6 percent).

The researchers found that treatment with Botox cut the number of headaches by more than half (56 percent), and also reduced the number of headache days per month from 18.9 days to 8.3 days. In addition, when the Botox subjects *did* get headaches, they were 25 percent less intense than they were pre-Botox. The researchers concluded, "These results suggest that botulinum toxin type A may be an effective and safe prophylactic treatment for a variety of moderate to severe chronic headache types."

chemical associated with pain, as well as glutamate and calcitonin gene-related peptide (CGRP), all neurochemicals associated with pain production.

Some experts believe that the resulting relaxation of the muscles after a Botox injection improves blood flow to the area, enabling endorphins—or natural painkillers—to provide further pain relief; and that may be a key mechanism by which Botox works. To most patients, however, it doesn't really matter *how* Botox works. It just matters that it *does* work.

Benefits of Botox Therapy

If Botox injections work, the primary benefit is that you have fewer headaches, and the ones that you still get are less intense. Another advantage is that you can have the shots in your doctor's office rather than needing to go to a surgery center or hospital, as is sometimes necessary when you have a nerve block or other procedures used to treat chronic head or neck pain. Another benefit: you'll probably be able to reduce your headache medication. Most medications have side effects, and if you can avoid pain medications, all the better—especially if you're taking narcotics.

Side Effects of Botox

Do the shots hurt? Those who've had them say they feel like pinpricks or a minor bug bite. Botox is generally safe and any side effects are usually temporary. Local reactions—including redness, soreness, and muscle irritation—are some of the minor side effects often seen with these injections.

Some patients report experiencing flulike symptoms, such as chills and fever, after their Botox injections. Others complain of muscle tenderness, and there may be some mild bruising at the injection site. A rash may develop at the injection site, and if it appears, it should go away in a few days. Some patients have temporary minor difficulty with swallowing (*dysphagia*) if shots are given near the throat area. Some patients who receive neck injections may experience neck weakness or a "stiff neck." Rarely, patients can experience a muscle weakness that can result in a head droop, which can be quite uncomfortable.

Some patients complain of a temporary increase in their headaches or their neck pain directly after having injections, which could be an effect of the needles or may mean that the Botox dose was too low.

Probably the most obvious complication of using Botox, and it's rare, is the risk of a drooping eyelid (*ptosis*), which may occur if the injections are not performed by an experienced doctor, or if the physician used too high a dosage for the face. Studies reported by cosmetic surgeons indicate this complication occurs in about 1–5 percent of patients receiving Botox in the forehead. As the Botox wears off, the problem abates.

Another side effect of Botox is that you may experience less facial flexibility than in the past. Your face shouldn't appear frozen, but if, for example, you're an actor who needs to show extremes of emotion, Botox shots may prevent your full range of expressions until the shots wear off, usually after a period of 4–8 weeks. (You'd need to consult a cosmetic surgeon to find out exactly how long Botox shots used to treat wrinkles could prevent a full range of facial expressions.)

Here are our suggestions when using Botox therapy for your headaches and for considering the side effects.

- Your doctor should talk to you about the possible complications and if she doesn't, ask for an explanation.
- Ask your doctor approximately how many patients she has used Botox on for headache treatment; and of these patients, how many had a problem with side effects and what they were.
- Seek a doctor who has injected at least 25 patients with Botox. Go for experience and don't let anyone *learn* how to use Botox on your face, head, or neck. As with any other technical procedure, the more the doctor has done, the more skillful he will be at performing the procedure.

Cost of Botox

The high cost of the drug is also a disadvantage, as Botox is pricey and its cost can be constraining. Since its use in headaches hasn't yet been approved by the Food and Drug Administration (FDA), some insurance companies refuse to pay for it. (But don't assume this is true for your health insurance company. Some insurance companies *are* paying for Botox.)

The cost for one 100–unit vial is about $550; and patients may need one to two vials for one set of injections. And don't forget, your physician will also charge a fee for performing the injections, on top of the cost of the drug. In considering the cost of both the Botox and your doctor's fees, one set of injections to treat chronic headaches can cost from $1,000 to $2,000 or more, depending on the doctor, how many areas you need injected, and other factors.

Insurance Matters. Some patients pay for the drug themselves, while health insurance companies pay for the drug for other patients. Before deciding whether they'll pay for your Botox injections, your insurance company may request more information from your physician, such as a letter stating that all therapies have failed for your chronic severe headaches, but that the doctor believes Botox may be effective for you. Your doctor should be willing to write such a letter, if he truly believes Botox would help you.

Sometimes the drug can be obtained at no cost for a headache patient, depending on the patient's circumstances. According to individuals at the Botox Reimbursement Hotline, a service associated with Allergan that provides phone assistance on insurance coverage for Botox, there are two patient-assistance programs. One program is for patients with no insurance, and it's run by the National Organization for Rare Diseases (NORD). Another program is for patients who have insurance, but whose insurance company refuses to cover Botox injections.

Patients who are approved for either program will receive the drug for free for one year. After the year is up, they may be eligible for reenrollment, depending on their circumstances. Keep in mind that it's the Botox that's free, not your doctor's fees. Also, free Botox won't be approved if it's for cosmetic purposes.

Note: It is apparently little known, but Botox may be covered under your pharmacy benefits, such that the doctor could write a prescription filled by your local pharmacy or a mail-order pharmacy. The drug may be received by the patient, who brings it to the doctor's office, or it may be mailed directly to the physician, depending on insurance coverage and the individual case.

Sometimes whether Botox is covered by insurance companies or Medicare depends on the diagnosis code the doctor uses. Although you may not realize it, whenever you go to the doctor, your illness is assigned a specific numerical diagnosis code, and it may affect whether the insurance company will pay the doctor. Doctors may use various diagnosis medication codes, such as intractable classic migraine (346.01), intractable common migraine (346.11), intractable variants of migraine (346.21), intractable other forms of headache (346.81), or intractable headache (784.0). These are only a few diagnosis codes used, and according to the Botox Reimbursement Hotline, there are over several hundred diagnosis codes that they support for Botox.

How Botox Is Used for Headaches: The Process

If you and your physician decide to use Botox to treat your headaches, the doctor will order the drug. She must mix up the Botox in the office, and after she does this, it's only good for about four hours. If there's any Botox left after the injections, it must be discarded by the physician. Sorry! It can't be saved for later.

Before Botox

Patients who will be receiving Botox injections should stop taking nonsteroidal anti-inflammatory drugs (NSAIDs) and vitamin E for about a week before they get their shots because NSAIDS and vitamin E can thin out the blood. There shouldn't be much (or any) bleeding from the injections, but doctors often wish to be extra careful. Other than this simple precaution, you don't have to do anything special beforehand. Just show up on time for your appointment! If you are particularly sensitive to injections, there are creams and topical agents that can be used to numb the skin over the areas to be injected.

Receiving Botox

The doctor will determine the location of your muscle pain and spasm through a physical examination. He may also use electromyography (EMG) equipment to identify small or delicate muscles that are spasming. An EMG uses a recording electrode that actually feels like a needle to measure the amount of muscle activity in a specific muscle. Too much activity is consistent with muscle spasm. We use EMG guidance for muscles that are small and sensitive, and we rely on the physical examination to determine muscle spasms of the larger muscles.

In general, the physician selects at least 8–9 sites where the Botox will be injected, although you may receive 20 or more injections. These areas are wiped clean before the needle is inserted. The doctor may also spray the area with a numbing medication beforehand, although the injections are not painful, since we use very small needles. Wearing surgical gloves to avoid contamination, the doctor smooths out the skin in the intended injection site and then injects the Botox. The most common injection sites for headache patients are between the eyebrows, in the forehead area, and in the neck. Depending on the doctor and where you'll receive the injections, you'll either be sitting up or lying down to receive the shots.

If the doctor plans to inject the corrugator muscle in the forehead (a common site for headache patients), he may ask you to frown so these muscles are easier for him to see and feel. If he will inject the Botox in the temporalis muscle, which is on the side of the head at the level of the eye, he may ask you to clench your teeth so he can see and feel these muscles better.

Some doctors use a "fixed site" approach to injections, which means that they inject only in the areas that are usually problems for people with chronic severe headaches. This means that even if your headache occurs on only one side, the doctor may inject the other corresponding side of your head as well. This is done to avoid the headache switching from one side to the other, as sometimes happens.

Note: Do not rub the areas where you were just injected because you could inadvertently spread the Botox outwards. You don't want this to happen, since you want the full concentrated effect of the drug in the areas where your head hurts.

Don't expect immediate results. It will take several days, and up to two weeks, for the full effect to occur and some patients don't gain the complete benefit until their second or third session. Also, don't expect a cure. You'll probably need more injections later on.

After Botox

You should see your doctor within about four weeks of receiving your Botox injections, for a follow-up visit. It's unlikely that you'll receive any more injections at this time, as the purpose of this visit is for you to tell the doctor if the shots helped. If your doctor has given you a headache diary to keep, bring it in. The headache diary is generally a simple record of the dates of when any headaches occurred and their intensity. You and your doctor can use this information to see how you're doing headache-wise, rather than relying on memory alone.

Our Experiences with Botox Headache Therapy

We started using Botox with our headache patients in 1999, and we treat about 300–400 headache patients per year with Botox. It has worked very well for our patients; about 70 percent have found dramatic relief from Botox that they didn't obtain from medications or other therapies they've tried.

We vary the number of injections and the area of the injection sites with the individual patient, although many patients with cervicogenic headaches also need injections in the neck and shoulder area. We've generally found that the first set of injections is effective for about 2–3 months. After the first one or two sets of injections, we've found the drug lasts 3–4 months, and then it lasts 4–6 months. Many of our headache patients consider Botox to be a miracle drug, even though it hasn't cured them forever. When you're in constant pain from severe headaches, something that makes you get fewer and less intense headaches really does seem like a miracle drug.

How to Find Out More About Botox and Headaches

Ask your doctor for more information about Botox. If he is unfamiliar with the therapy, you can go to the Allergan website for patient information at botox.com. This site offers information on Botox in general as well as on insurance coverage for treatment.

Patients can also call the Botox Reimbursement Hotline at 800-530-6680 to be evaluated for possible coverage for injections.

If you have insurance, you'll need to give them permission to contact your health insurance company to find out if they'll cover Botox injections for your headaches. It takes about two months for the Botox Reimbursement Hotline to determine if you're eligible for insurance coverage or a patient assistance program; and each person is evaluated on a case-by-case basis. They also provide assistance with denied claims. (Remember that just because your insurance company says no, that doesn't necessarily mean it's a "no" forever.)

In the last chapter of this book, we provide you with information on alternative therapies for treating and preventing your chronic headaches. In addition, we offer suggestions for lifestyle changes to prevent their frequency.

CHAPTER 13

Alternative Therapies and What You Can Do to Prevent Chronic Headaches

It's important to gain significant relief from the acutely painful headache that you have right now. But it's also a good idea to make changes in your life that can help you *prevent* cluster headaches, tension-type headaches, and the other headaches that we discussed in previous chapters from happening in the first place. That's the purpose of this chapter.

In addition to providing general advice on preventing chronic headaches, such as resolving stress problems, getting enough sleep, and avoiding food triggers, you'll also find information on alternative therapies to treat your chronic headaches. Many of these options, such as electrical stimulation and relaxation therapy, work well for virtually all headache patients. Other options, such as acupuncture, seem to work best for patients with migraine headaches, although patients with tension-type or cervicogenic headaches may also benefit. Also, be sure to read our suggestions for preventing cervicogenic headaches in Chapter 6—even if you don't have them—because many of the ideas that we describe there will work well for people with other types of headaches, too.

For example, many patients with cervicogenic headaches have benefited significantly from chiropractic treatment; and other chronic headache patients might find this type of treatment helpful as well.

Biofeedback and neurofeedback are other options that may help you to prevent or at least decrease the number of your chronic severe headaches. In addition, learning tai chi or yoga exercises may also dramatically lower your stress level, and by doing so, enable you to significantly decrease the number of your headaches.

Get Any Other Medical Problems Treated

Of course, the first step, if you have any other underlying medical problems, is to get those problems treated. We know it sounds obvious, but it's important, so we want to emphasize it here. If there's a chance that you could have diabetes, thyroid disease, or another medical problem that's causing your headaches, then see your doctor to obtain a diagnosis and get the problem treated and, if possible, resolved. Don't forget that certain medications can cause or exacerbate headaches, so if you have concerns, discuss them with your doctor. A *Physicians' Desk Reference* can also be helpful, as it is a reference book of all prescription and many nonprescription drugs.

It's also important that you see the appropriate type of doctor to obtain the best treatment. For example, the endocrinologist is the best expert to treat metabolic problems like thyroid disease or diabetes. If you have chronic sinus headaches from sinusitis, see an otolaryngologist (ear, nose, and throat doctor) to help you resolve the problem. When the headaches may stem from an eye problem, see an ophthalmologist. Of course, neurologists are the best doctors for brain pain.

Reduce Your Stress Levels

If your headaches could be related to extreme chronic stress, you may wish to see a psychiatrist or psychologist. And please note that you don't have to have a severe problem such as a multiple personality disorder or schizophrenia in order to see a mental health expert. Psychiatrists and psychologists routinely treat people who hold down jobs and are basically mentally healthy, but who need to develop better coping mechanisms because their stress is overburdening them.

We're not saying that your pain isn't real and that you've somehow imagined it. Instead, extreme stress definitely tenses up muscles and causes changes in many chemicals and hormones in the body. Sometimes medication and various other headache therapies that you try aren't quite enough when you're really stressed out; and you may need to obtain help with what's been stressing you out so much in the first place.

Stress is a major headache inducer for nearly every chronic headache type, so when you find effective ways to reduce stress, it usually follows that your headaches will also decrease in their frequency and intensity. Of course, what works well for one person won't work at all for another; but in general, there are effective actions that you can take to improve your stress levels, such as learning how to perform progressive muscle relaxation therapy, getting enough sleep, and identifying and avoiding your food triggers.

Progressive Muscle-Relaxation Therapy

Many over-stressed people obtain major depressurizing stress relief through progressive muscle-relaxation therapy. In one study described in a 1994 issue of *Gastroenterology*, patients who were suffering from chronic acid reflux were actually able to reduce the amount of their stomach acidity through progressive muscle-relaxation training, and consequently, they felt better. In fact, many of the subjects had a normal level of acidity after completing their relaxation therapy training.

How did the researchers know how acidic the stomachs of the subjects were? Using special devices that they had inserted into the patients' stomachs, the researchers were able to measure the stomach acid of the relaxation therapy group before and after training. To make the test even more challenging, the subjects had been given acid-inducing foods to eat, such as pizza and soft drinks.

Of course, your problem isn't acid reflux (although you may have that problem as well)—you suffer from chronic headaches. But here's the thing: If relaxation therapy can help people cut back on their stomach acid, doesn't it also make sense that it could help you better manage your chronic headaches? We think that it does.

To learn how to perform progressive muscle-relaxation therapy, you can see a therapist, such as a physical therapist or a psychologist, for instructions. (Call first to find out if the therapist offers relaxation training. Therapists vary in the methods that they use to help patients.) Or you could buy books or audiotapes in your local bookstore or online. Basically, the technique involves lying down and concentrating on one part of your body, and imagining all the stress and tension flowing outward. Some people start this mental exercise by imagining their feet relaxing totally, then their knees, their lower torso, and so forth as they work their way up to their heads. Others start at the top and do a stepwise relaxation downwards. Either way is fine.

Relaxation therapy may sound silly and even like a waste of time to some people; but unfortunately, these are often the people who need it the most! You may worry that you could fall asleep at the end of a relaxation session, and this is true. You can. So don't schedule any high-powered meetings or an appointment with your child's teacher for right after your relaxation-therapy session. You might be a little *too* laid back for those activities. Instead, set aside time in the day, perhaps after dinner, for at least 30 minutes of relaxation therapy.

It's also interesting to note that when you aren't so worried and upset, often the answers to problems that have been troubling you will come to the forefront of your brain with a marked clarity. This shouldn't be the goal of performing relaxation therapy but it may be another benefit.

Sleep: Are You Getting Enough?

If you're getting five or six hours of sleep per night (or less), it's just not enough. The body literally regenerates in the evening when you're asleep, and there are hormones—that are produced at night—that work to replenish your body and alleviate the damage that time and stress has done to you. Dreams may also play a role in clearing out the psychic cobwebs, and studies have shown that people who are deprived of dreaming will eventually become extremely agitated and irrational.

When you shortchange your body with a lack of sleep or create a constant sleep deficit because of stress, sleep apnea, or some other problem, often you risk developing a chronic headache problem. Of course, not everyone who fails to sleep enough gets headaches. Some people get stomachaches, back pain, or another medical problem. The payback has to come from somewhere.

If you are acquiring a "sleep debt," it will need to be paid back. We don't care that you used to pull all-nighters when you were in high school or college, cramming before your final exams. That wasn't a good idea then and now that you're an adult, it's a really bad idea. Get some sleep! And if you're an insomniac, look at Chapter 11 again for information on melatonin, a supplement that can make you sleepy.

Identify and Avoid Your Food Triggers

In Chapter 3, we talked about many different triggers for headaches, how you can use a headache diary to help you identify your particular food triggers, and how you can try eliminating or greatly cutting back on the food triggers that are the most common to see if you notice any difference in the frequency and severity of your headaches. (Hopefully, there'll be fewer of them and the ones that you do get won't hurt you as much!) Common headache triggers for many people with chronic headaches include anything that contains caffeine (such as coffee, tea, or most soft drinks) as well as alcohol and cheese. You should also avoid foods that contain monosodium glutamate (MSG), which is a food additive.

Finding Relief with Alternative Therapies

Medications are often the mainstay for people with chronic severe headaches. However, there are also other options to choose from whether you have an active headache, an emerging one, or you're trying to hold your frequent headaches at bay. Some people benefit from acupuncture, some from electrical stimulation, and others from doing yoga or tai chi. In addition, biofeedback or neurofeedback can provide significant relief for many people with chronic headaches, particularly patients with cervicogenic ones.

Biofeedback

It probably sounds very New Age–ish, but biofeedback can be very effective in helping some patients control their chronic headaches. Biofeedback is a noninvasive therapy in which, with the help of a therapist or a technician, you use a computer to learn to control some of your basic body processes—such as slightly lowering your body temperature (and by doing so, inducing a more calm state), pulse, and/or heart rate. A typical session lasts about 30 minutes. Simple sensors that will monitor your vital signs are placed on your skin, and they easily peel off at the end of a session. With biofeedback, you'll view minute changes in your temperature, pulse, or other measurements on a computer screen, and note these changes as you tense up or relax. By viewing their reactions on the monitor, many people can develop the ability to change them, which leads to greater relaxation.

The theory behind biofeedback is that if you are able to successfully lower your skin temperature, blood pressure, pulse, heart rate, and other vital signs, then you will subsequently feel more relaxed, and you will also be less likely to develop severe headaches that are caused by stress. Stress often causes a "fight/flight" response in the body, which is why all your vital signs accelerate under stress. You run away (either literally or figuratively, and this happens more often as your stress levels go up) from things that really bother you, or you stand and fight. More frequently, instead of a physical caveman-like confrontation, you verbally argue with or confront whoever is causing you stress. This makes your hormonal stress levels skyrocket. Constant periods of these fight/ flight reactions lead to chronic stress and anxiety as well as to physical symptoms, such as recurrent headaches.

Biofeedback, when it works, doesn't deal directly with whatever is stressing you out; but instead, it helps you concentrate and change your body's responses to stressors. When you can control your reactions, even though the stressors are still there, you will not feel as upset. You'll still have emotions, of course, and won't become a zombie-like person. You'll continue to become happy or upset, as appropriate, and your vital signs will change when you're joyful or despondent. But if it works, you'll gain better control over your day-to-day reactions to everyday events.

Biofeedback does not work for everyone, however; and some hard-driving "Type A" people may have a difficult time mastering this therapy because they may be fixated on action and achievement, when the essence of biofeedback is basically letting go and relaxing. While it isn't for everyone, it can be very helpful for many people with chronic headaches. You can't know if it'll work for you until you've tried it for at least several sessions. Interestingly, some research indicates that the relaxation techniques that are learned during biofeedback sessions can be drawn upon later when people are far away from the computer.

This means that if you master biofeedback, you'll have another tool to use when you become overstressed to help you decrease your risk of developing a headache or an even worse medical problem.

Another form of biofeedback is *electromyography* (*EMG*) biofeedback, in which special sensors measure and display the tension on specific muscles. Consequently, you learn to relax the affected muscles; particularly the muscles in the face, neck, or the shoulders. EMG feedback has been demonstrated to be the most effective in treating tension-type headaches. In many cases, patients first receive training in progressive muscle relaxation therapy, which is then followed by EMG biofeedback.

If you're interested in either form of biofeedback, ask your doctor if he can recommend an expert in your area to help you get started. Some physicians, such as neurologists, offer biofeedback, as do some psychologists and physical therapists. We employ this modality frequently in patients with head, neck, or back pain and even in patients with anxiety. It is truly an empowering technology and allows the individual to control body processes that are usually not under voluntary control.

Neurofeedback

A newer therapy than biofeedback, *neurofeedback*, may also provide you with considerable pain relief and serve as a preventive measure against future headaches. Neurofeedback uses an *electroencephalograph* (*EEG*), which is a device that measures the patient's brain waves via electrodes placed on specific areas of the scalp. With neurofeedback, patients view their own brain waves on the screen, and when it works, they can consciously alter the brain waves. By doing so, they will decrease the frequency and severity of their headaches. EEG neurofeedback is also used to treat other conditions, such as depression, sleep disorders, and attention-deficit/hyperactivity disorder (ADHD) in adolescents and adults. Since many people with chronic headaches have depression and/or sleep disorders, neurofeedback could provide multiple benefits. It may also help you pay attention more, whether you have ADHD or not!

However, neurofeedback is a relatively new and controversial therapy, and one we don't yet offer to our patients. Some doctors favor it while others remain skeptical. The therapy may be available through a neurologist in your area or who is associated with a medical school at a large university. Because neurofeedback is considered an experimental therapy by most health insurance companies, you'll probably have to cover the cost yourself.

Pinning Down Your Pain: Acupuncture

Studies are mixed on whether acupuncture is effective at reducing most types of chronic headaches, but some patients insist that they have gained dramatic relief. However, when it comes to migraines and tension-type headaches, studies have demonstrated that acupuncture *does* help to decrease the frequency and severity of migraines. Acupuncture may help with cervicogenic headaches, too.

What is acupuncture? It's the use of tiny needles, which are inserted directly into the skin at specific points. Another form of acupuncture is *electroacupuncture*, which is acupuncture that uses needles to deliver electrical impulses.

Acupuncture is based on a rather complicated Chinese theory, but many modern physicians believe that what actually happens when acupuncture works is that the needles stimulate the production of endorphins, natural painkillers that surge to the area that's being stimulated, which is also the area that hurts you. Sometimes the relief can be quite dramatic.

Many acupuncturists are not medical doctors, however; and we believe it's best to receive your therapy from a physician or from a certified acupuncturist who is well versed in the specialty. If you're considering acupuncture, ask your doctor if she can recommend a physician in your area or another licensed practitioner who performs acupuncture.

Clinical Studies in Using Acupuncture to Treat Headaches

In one study of 401 patients in England and Wales, most of them with migraines (discussed in a 2004 issue of *British Medical Journal*), the study patients received acupuncture over a three-month period, and their results were compared to a control group of headache patients who received standard care.

The findings: The acupuncture group experienced a 34 percent reduction in their headaches, compared to the control group, which experienced a 16 percent reduction. In addition, the patients in the acupuncture group used significantly less medication (15 percent less), took fewer sick days off (again, 15 percent), and made fewer visits to their doctors (25 percent less). According to the researchers, "Acupuncture leads to persisting, clinically relevant benefits for primary care patients with chronic headache, particularly migraine."

In another study, reported in a 2004 issue of *Headache*, patients were given electroacupuncture. A small group of only 37 patients in the study and control group were studied, and the researchers found that electroacupuncture was effective in providing short-term relief for patients with tension-type headaches. A significant number of the study patients experienced reduced headache attacks that were less intense; and the improvement continued for six weeks or more.

Electrical Stimulation ("E-Stim")

Some people with chronic headaches have tried medications, acupuncture, and other therapies and they still have received little or no relief from their pain. Then they tried *electrical stimulation*—often referred to by doctors as "e-stim," for short—and it worked very well for them. Electrical stimulation is helpful to some patients and doesn't work at all in others; and no one knows why. In general, electrical stimulation may work best for patients with tension-type headaches and/or musculoskeletal pain, such as is found with cervicogenic headaches, rather than for patients with other headache types.

Don't confuse electrical stimulation therapy with the pain of an electric shock. Electrical stimulation therapy should provide you with mild stimulation that you can feel, yet it isn't painful. If it *is* painful, then the setting is too high!

You may be able to obtain electrical stimulation therapy from your physician, or he may refer you to a physical therapist for treatment. In some cases, your doctor may recommend that you use a home unit to help you control your headache pain as well as pain that you may have in the neck and back.

Transcutaneous electrical stimulation (TENS) or *percutaneous electrical nerve stimulation (PENS)* electrical impulse are the two primary forms of electrical stimulation therapy used to treat frequent headaches. With TENS, electrodes are placed at specific sites on the body in order to deliver low levels of electrical current. PENS uses needles rather than electrodes to deliver the electrical impulses that can provide you with pain control. Some studies have shown that with tension-type headaches, migraines, and other headaches, PENS therapy significantly reduced the patients' headache pain. It also improved their sleep quality and, in addition, their physical activity level during the day was higher than before the PENS therapy was given.

Neither TENS nor PENS therapy should be used in patients who have had heart pacemakers installed, because these therapies may interfere with the patient's pacemaker, and could even cause it to deliver unneeded shocks to the user.

Yoga and Tai Chi

Many people are able to obtain a state of calmness and serenity through performing exercises that are a part of either yoga or tai chi. Tai chi is a form of Chinese martial arts that involves exercises that simulate the movements of animals, such as a crane or a snake. Yoga has its own set of specific exercises, and, as with tai chi, you start at a beginner level. As you master the movements or exercises, you eventually progress to more difficult ones. Both tai chi and yoga can provide individuals with a feeling of control and calm. Calmness doesn't always mean you'll have no further headaches, but please keep in mind that the reverse is often true: extreme stress *does* increase your risk for headaches.

If you belong to a gym, many offer classes in tai chi or various kinds of yoga in addition to all other sorts of classes as part of your membership. In addition, many community centers offer inexpensive or free classes in yoga and tai chi, so you should check to see if and when classes are held in your area. Many community colleges offer low-cost courses in yoga or tai chi for local residents. You usually don't have to take tests or formally apply to the school to take classes. You just fill out a few forms, pay the fees, and show up for classes, often held at night or on weekends for your convenience.

Concluding Remarks

We've now come to the end of our book journey with you, and we hope that our sharing with you what we know about chronic and severe headaches, based on our own professional experience with thousands of headache patients as well as our extensive review of current medical research on headaches, has given you important tools to help you combat your aggravating and painful headaches.

Maybe you've discovered that the cause of your headaches was a particular food that you now avoid (like red wine or aged cheese), or it's a chemical or food additive (like caffeine or monosodium glutamate) that you'll steer clear of from now on. Maybe you found out that your headache type was misdiagnosed and that you really suffer from cervicogenic headaches (that were diagnosed as migraines) or migraines (that were diagnosed as sinus headaches), and a new look at your symptoms with your physician has facilitated an accurate diagnosis and treatment that works for you.

Perhaps before you read our book, you didn't know about exercises or chiropractic treatments that could help with cervicogenic headaches, or Botox treatments that can ease the pain of migraines. You may not have known about therapies that can help you, such as biofeedback or acupuncture. You may have learned about prescribed medications designed specifically for headaches; medications that are used for other illnesses but that are also effective in treating headaches; or supplements and vitamins that can help many people with headaches, such as riboflavin, magnesium, and melatonin.

It may not have occurred to you that your own actions, such as lugging around a heavy purse or briefcase or the way you cradle the phone to your ear with your shoulder hunched up could be contributing to your headaches, and that changing these behaviors can bring you significant relief.

Whatever messages you take away from our book, we hope that they will guide you in the right direction to rid yourself of your headaches altogether or at least dramatically decrease their frequency and intensity. As physicians with a keen interest in headaches, we know that headache pain can devastate people's lives, and we also know that alleviating that pain can turn around those same lives.

Please also keep in mind that increasing numbers of physicians are starting to realize that chronic severe headaches are important problems, just as are other chronic medical problems, such as hypertension, thyroid disease, or diabetes. (And sometimes people *with* untreated hypertension, thyroid disease, or diabetes suffer from chronic headaches.) You deserve acknowledgment of your pain and suffering, as well as information on ways to overcome that pain. Work with a doctor who accepts that chronic headache pain is real, and who thinks that it's important to tailor the solution to the individual patient.

Don't let anyone tell you that you must suffer from chronic headaches and that you'll just have to learn to live with it. In almost all cases, that is not true. We hope that our book has made clear to you that most patients with chronic headaches can recover, so that you now look forward to a more headache-free future.

Bibliography

Ahmed, Hesham E., et al. "Use of Percutaneous Electrical Nerve Stimulation (PENS) in the Short-Term Management of Headache," *Headache* 40 (2000): 311–315.

Anthony, M. "Cervicogenic Headache: Prevalence and Response to Local Steroid Therapy," *Clinical and Experimental Rheumatology* 2, Supplement 19 (2000): S49–S64.

Bigal, Marcelo E., et al. "Chronic Daily Headache: Identification of Factors Associated with Induction and Transformation," *Headache* 42 (2002): 575–581.

Biondi, David M. "Cervicogenic Headache: Mechanisms, Evaluation, and Treatment Strategies," *Journal of the American Osteopathic Association* 100, no. 9 (Supplement to September 2000): S7–S13.

Blumenfeld, Andrew M. "Botulinum Toxin Type A as an Effective Prophylactic Treatment in Primary Headache Disorders," *Headache: The Journal of Head and Face Pain* 43, no. 8 (September 2003): 853–860.

Blumenfeld, Andrew M., et al. "Procedures for Administering Botulinum Toxin Type A for Migraine and Tension-Type Headache," *Headache* 43 (2003): 884–889.

Blumenthal, Harvey J. "Headaches and Sinus Disease," *Headache* 41 (2001): 883–888.

Brandes, Jan Lewis, et al. "Topiramate for Migraine Prevention: A Randomized Controlled Trial," *Journal of the American Medical Association* 291, no. 8 (2004): 965–973.

Cady, Roger, et al. "Migraine Treatment with Rizatriptan and Non-Triptan Usual Care Medications: A Pharmacy-Based Study," *Headache* 44 (2004): 900–907.

Case, Allison M., and Robert L. Reid. "Effects of the Menstrual Cycle on Medical Disorders," *Archives of Internal Medicine* 158 (1998): 1405–1412.

Colas, R., et al. "Chronic Daily Headache with Analgesic Overuse: Epidemiology and Impact on Quality of Life," *Neurology* 62 (2004): 1338–1342.

Demirkaya, Seref, et al. "Efficacy of Intravenous Magnesium Sulfate in the Treatment of Acute Migraine Attacks," *Headache* 41 (2001): 171–177.

Dowson, Andrew J., et al. "Zolmitriptan Nasal Spray Exhibits Good Long-Term Safety and Tolerability in Migraine: Results of the INDEX Trial," *Headache* 45 (2005): 17–24.

Dumas, J. P., et al. "Physical Impairments in Cervicogenic Headache: Traumatic vs. Nontraumatic Onset," *Cephalgia* 21 (2001): 884–893.

Edmeads, John G. "Disorders of the Neck: Cervicogenic Headache," in Wolff's *Headache and Other Head Pain*. Seventh Edition. New York: Oxford University Press, 2001.

Ferrone, Marcus, and Susannah Motl. "Current Pharmacotherapy for the Treatment of Migraine," *U.S. Pharmacist* 28, no. 3 (2003), uspharmacist.com/index.asp?show=article&page=8_1039.htm, retrieved November 18, 2004.

Fishbain, David A., et al. "International Headache Society Diagnostic Patterns in Pain Facility Patients," *Clinical Journal of Pain* 17 (2001): 78–93.

Freund, Brian J., et al. "Treatment of Chronic Cervical-Associated Headache with Botulinum Toxin A: A Pilot Study," *Headache* 40, no. 3 (2000): 231–236.

Fricton, James R. "Temperomandibular Muscle and Joint Disorders," *Pain: Clinical Updates* 12, no. 2 (2004): 1–6.

Goadsby, Peter J., Richard B. Lipton, and Michel Ferrai. "Migraine—Current Understanding and Treatment," *New England Journal of Medicine* 346, no. 4 (2002): 257–270.

Hering-Hanit, R., N. Gadoth. "Caffeine-Induced Headache in Children and Adolescents," *Cephalgia* 23, no. 4 (2003): 332.

Jankovic, J. "Botulinum Toxin in Clinical Practice," *Journal of Neurology, Neurosurgery, and Psychiatry* 75 (2004): 951–957.

Jousilahti, Pekka, et al. "Headache and the Risk of Stroke: A Prospective Observational Cohort Study Among 35,056 Finnish Men and Women," *Archives of Internal Medicine* 163 (2003): 1058–1062.

Jull, Gwendolen, et al. "A Randomized Controlled Trial of Exercise and Manipulative Therapy for Cervicogenic Headache," *Spine* 27, no. 17 (2002): 1835–1843.

Kandel, Joseph, and David B. Sudderth. *Migraine: What Works!* (Rocklin, CA: Prima Publishing), 2000.

Kaniecki, Robert. "Headache Assessment and Management," *Journal of the American Medical Association* 289, no. 11 (2003): 1430–1433.

Kelman, Leslie. "Osmophobia and Taste Abnormality in Migraineurs: A Tertiary Care Study," *Headache* 44 (2004): 1019–1023.

Kelman, Leslie. "The Premonitory Symptoms (Prodrome): A Tertiary Care Study of 893 Migraineurs," *Headache* 44 (2004): 865–872.

Kelman, Leslie. "Women's Issues of Migraine in Tertiary Care," *Headache* 44 (2004): 2–7.

Lipton, Richard B., et al. "Sumatriptan Relieves Migrainelike Headaches Associated with Carbon Monoxide Exposure," *Headache* 37, no. 6 (1997): 392–395.

Loh, N. K. et al. "Do Patients with Obstructive Sleep Apnea Wake Up with Headaches?" *Archives of Internal Medicine* 159 (1999): 1765–1768.

MacGregor, E. Anne, Jan Brandes, and Astrid Eikermann. "Migraine Prevalence and Treatment Patterns: The Global Migraine and Zolmitriptan Evaluation Survey," *Headache* 43 (2003): 19–26.

Manchikanti, Laxmalah. "Neural Blockade in Cervical Pain Syndromes," *Pain Physician* 21, no. 3 (1999): 65–84.

Marcus, Dawn A. "Gender Differences in Treatment-Seeking Chronic Headache Sufferers," *Headache* 41 (2001): 698–703.

Mauskop, Alexander. "Nutrition and Headache," American Council for Headache Education, achenet.org/articles/45.php, retrieved November 15, 2004.

Mauskop, Alexander, Bella T. Altura, and Burton M. Altura. "Serum Magnesium Levels and Serum Ionized Calcium/Ionized Magnesium Ratios in Women with Menstrual Migraine," *Headache* 42 (2002): 242–248.

McDonald-Haile, J., et al. "Relaxation Training Reduces Symptom Reports and Acid Exposure in Patients with Gastroesophageal Reflux Disease," *Gastroenterology* 107, no. 1 (1994): 61–69.

Minocha, Anil, and Christine Adamec. *The Encyclopedia of the Digestive System and Digestive Disorders.* New York: Facts On File, Inc., 2004.

Mueller, Loretta. "Tension-Type, the Forgotten Headache," *Postgraduate Medicine Online* 111, no. 4 (2002), postgradmed.com/issues/2002/04_02/mueller.htm, retrieved on November 18, 2004.

Nilsson, N. "The Prevalence of Cervicogenic Headache in a Random Population Sample of 20–59 Year Olds," *Spine* 20 (1995): 1884–1888.

Otte, A., et al. "PET and SPECT in Whiplash Syndrome: A New Approach to a Forgotten Brain?" *Journal of Neurology, Neurosurgery, and Psychiatry* 63, no. 3 (1997): 68–372.

Park, Jung Yul, et al. "Clinical Efficacy of Radiofrequency Cervical Zygapophyseal Neurotomy in Patients with Chronic Cervicogenic Headache," *Pain News* (Spring 2004): 6, 9–10.

Peres, et al. "Melatonin, 3 mg, Is Effective for Migraine Prevention," *Neurology* 63 (2004): 757.

Pfaffenrath, V., et al. "Magnesium in the Prophylaxis of Migraine: A Double-Blind, Placebo-Controlled Study," *Cephalgia* 16, no. 6 (1996): 436.

Prince, Patricia B., et al. "The Effect of Weather on Headache," *Headache* 44 (2004): 596–602.

Sandberg, Jared, "Let the Sun Shine In? Fluorescents Drive Some Workers Batty," *Wall Street Journal Online* (June 9, 2004): B1, retrieved on November 16, 2004.

Scarupa, Mark D., et al. "Rhinitis and Rhinologic Headaches," *Allergy and Asthma Proceedings* 25, no. 2 (2004): 101–105.

Schreiber, Curtis P. "Prevalence of Migraine in Patients with a History of Self-Reported or Physician-Diagnosed 'Sinus' Headache," *Archives of Internal Medicine* 164 (September 13, 2004): 1769–1772.

Sheedy, James E. *ErgoKit: Ergonomic Solutions for Comfortable Computing.* Dedham, Massachusetts: AliMed, 1994.

Silberstein, Stephen D., and Douglas C. McCrory. "Butalbital in the Treatment of Headache: History, Pharmacology, and Efficacy," *Headache* 41 (2001): 953–967.

Silberstein, Stephen D., and Douglas C. McCrory. "Ergotamine and Dihydroergotamine: History, Pharmacology, and Efficacy," *Headache* 43 (2003): 144–166.

Silberstein, Stephen D., et al. "A Randomized Trial of Frovatriptan for the Intermittent Prevention of Menstrual Migraine," *Neurology* 63 (2004): 261–269.

Silberstein, Stephen D., and John Rothrock, Guest Editors. *The State of Migraine: Prevention and Treatment.* Arlington Heights, Illinois: ACCESS Medical Group Department of Continuing Education, 2002.

Sjaastad, O., et al. "Cervicogenic Headache: Diagnostic Criteria," *Headache* 38 (1998): 442–445.

Sjaastad, O., T. A. Fredriksen, and V. Pfaffenrath. "Cervicogenic Headache: Diagnostic Criteria," *Headache* 30 (199): 725–726.

Slipman, C. W., et al. "Therapeutic Zygapophyseal Joint Injections for Headaches Emanating from the C2-3 Joint," *American Journal of Physical Medicine & Rehabilitation* 80, no. 3 (2001): 182–188.

Smetana, Gerald W. "The Diagnostic Value of Historical Features in Primary Headache Syndromes: A Comprehensive Review," *Archives of Internal Medicine* 160 (2000): 2729–2737.

Stewart, Walter F., et al. "Lost Productive Time and Cost Due to Common Pain Conditions in the US Workforce," *Journal of the American Medical Association* 290, no. 18 (November 12, 2003): 2443–2454.

Stewart, W. F., et al. "Menstrual Cycle and Headache in a Population Sample of Migraineurs," *Neurology* 55 (2000): 1517–1523.

Tepper, Stewart J., et al. "Prevalence and Diagnosis of Migraine in Patients Consulting Their Physician with a Complaint of Headache: Data from the Landmark Study," *Headache* 44 (2004): 856–864.

Vanagaite Vingen, Jolanta, Trond Sand, and Lars Jacob Stover. "Sensitivity to Various Stimuli in Primary Headaches: A Questionnaire Study," *Headache* 39 (September 1999): 552–558.

Van Het Loo, Mirjam, et al. *A Review of the Literature on Whiplash Associated Disorders.* The Netherlands: Rand Europe, 2002.

Vickers, Andrew J., et al. "Acupuncture for Chronic Headache in Primary Care: Large, Pragmatic, Randomised Trial," *British Medical Journal* 328 (2004): 744–747.

Wacogne, C., et al. "Stress, Anxiety, Depression and Migraine," *Cephalgia* 23, no. 6 (2003): 451.

Warner, John S. "The Outcome of Treating Patients with Suspected Rebound Headache," *Headache* 41 (2001): 685–692.

Weathermon, Ron, and David W. Crabb. "Alcohol and Medication Interactions," *Alcohol Research & Health* 23, no. 1 (1999).

Wenzel, Richard. "Migraine Headache Misconceptions: Barriers to Effective Care," *Pharmacotherapy* 24, no. 5 (2004): 638–648.

World Health Organization, "Headache Disorders," March 2004, who.int/mediacentre/factsheets/fs277/en/, retrieved on December 6, 2004.

Xue, C. C. L., et al. "Electroacupuncture for Tension-Type Headache on Distal Acupoints Only: A Randomized, Controlled, Crossover Trial," *Headache* 44 (2004): 333–341.

Zwart, J. A., et al. "Analgesic Overuse among Subjects with Headache, Neck, and Low-Back Pain," *Neurology* 62 (2004): 1540–1544.

Zwart, John-Anker. "Neck Mobility in Different Headache Disorders," *Headache* 37 (1997): 6–11.

Index

About the Authors

Joseph Kandel, M.D., is the founder and medical director of Neuroscience and Spine Associates, based in Naples, Florida, with offices in Fort Myers and Port Charlotte, Florida. He also is an associate clinical professor at Wright State University of Medicine. Dr. Kandel graduated from Wright State University School of Medicine and received his diplomate certification in neurology. He began his private practice in 1989 and is licensed to practice medicine in Florida and California.

In addition to multiple books coauthored with Dr. Sudderth, Dr. Kandel coauthored *The Encyclopedia of Senior Health and Well-Being* with Christine Adamec (Facts On File, Inc., 2002), and coauthored articles for prestigious medical journals, such as *Neurology*. He is a member of the American Medical Association, Florida Medical Association, American Academy of Neurology, the American Back Society, American Society of Neuroimaging, and Florida Society of Neurology.

David Sudderth, M.D., is in practice with Dr. Kandel, with whom he has been associated since 1992. Dr. Sudderth graduated from medical school at the University of Copenhagen and performed his internship and neurology residency at the Medical College of Wisconsin and at Emory University. He became a diplomate in psychiatry and neurology and received board recognition in pain management. He is licensed to practice medicine in Florida.

Dr. Sudderth is a member of the American Academy of Neurology, American Society of Neuroimaging, American Society of Pain Management, and Southern Medical Society. Dr. Sudderth is a popular public speaker on neurology topics and has been a guest physician on live Internet programs as well as broadcast television programs.

Dr. Kandel and Dr. Sudderth are the authors of *Back Pain: What Works!* (Prima Publishing, 1996), *Migraine: What Works!* (Prima Publishing, 2000), *Adult ADD: The Complete Handbook* (Prima Publishing, 1996), and several other self-help books. They have also produced self-help videotapes to help patients with migraines, back pain, and carpal tunnel syndrome. Both physicians have successfully treated thousands of patients with severe chronic headache problems, including cervicogenic headaches, migraines, and every other form of chronic headache.